Charles Wellbeloved

A Hand-Book to the Antiquities

in the grounds and museum of the Yorkshire Philosophical Society. Seventh Edition

Charles Wellbeloved

A Hand-Book to the Antiquities
in the grounds and museum of the Yorkshire Philosophical Society. Seventh Edition

ISBN/EAN: 9783337186999

Printed in Europe, USA, Canada, Australia, Japan

Cover: Foto ©Andreas Hilbeck / pixelio.de

More available books at **www.hansebooks.com**

A HAND-BOOK

TO THE

ANTIQUITIES

IN THE GROUNDS AND MUSEUM

OF THE

YORKSHIRE PHILOSOPHICAL SOCIETY.

BY THE LATE

REV. CHARLES WELLBELOVED,

WITH

LARGE ADDITIONS AND CORRECTIONS BY HIS SUCCESSORS IN THE OFFICE
OF CURATOR OF ANTIQUITIES.

SEVENTH EDITION.

YORK:

JOHN SAMPSON, PUBLISHER, CONEY STREET.

—

1881.

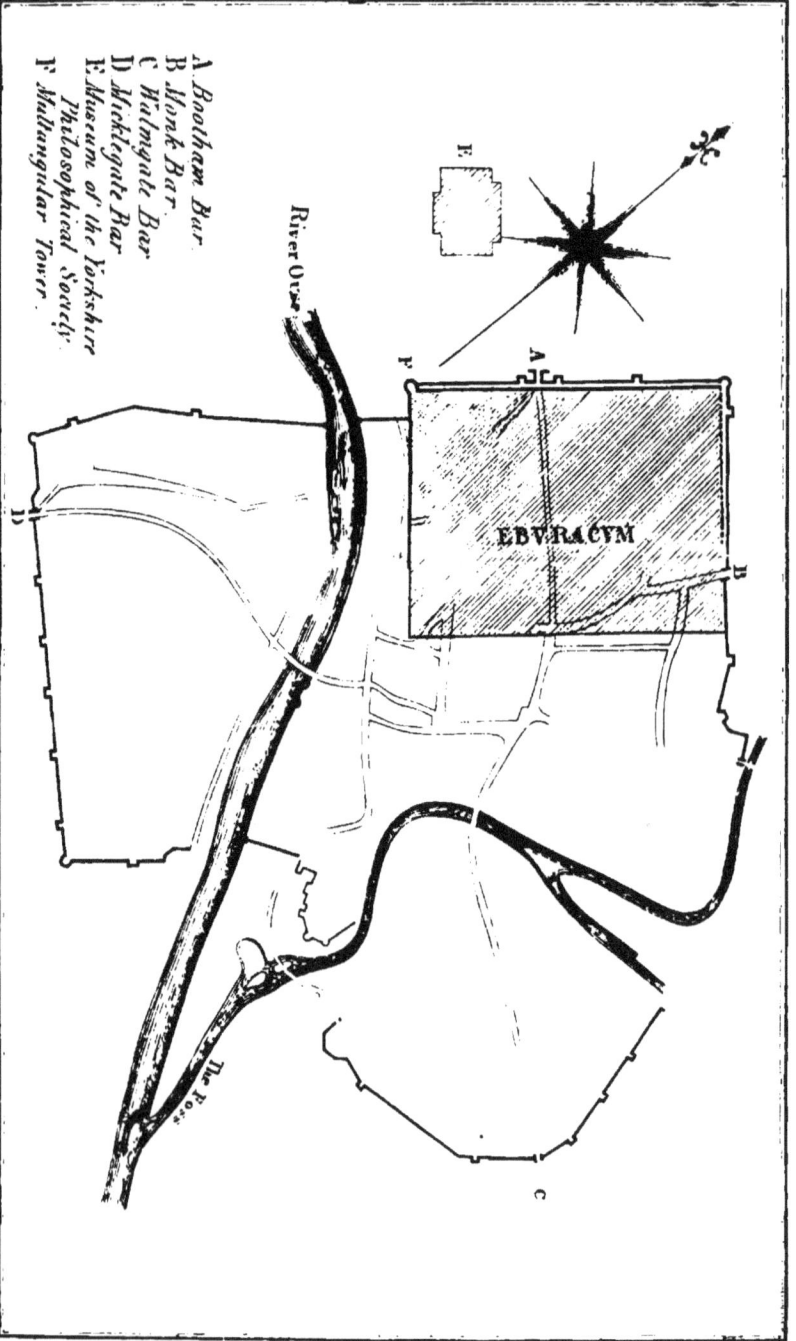

PLAN OF ANCIENT EBVRACVM AND MODERN YORK.

A. Bootham Bar.
B. Monk Bar.
C. Walmgate Bar.
D. Micklegate Bar.
E. Museum of the Yorkshire
   Philosophical Society.
F. Multangular Tower.

River Ouse

EBVRACVM

The Foss

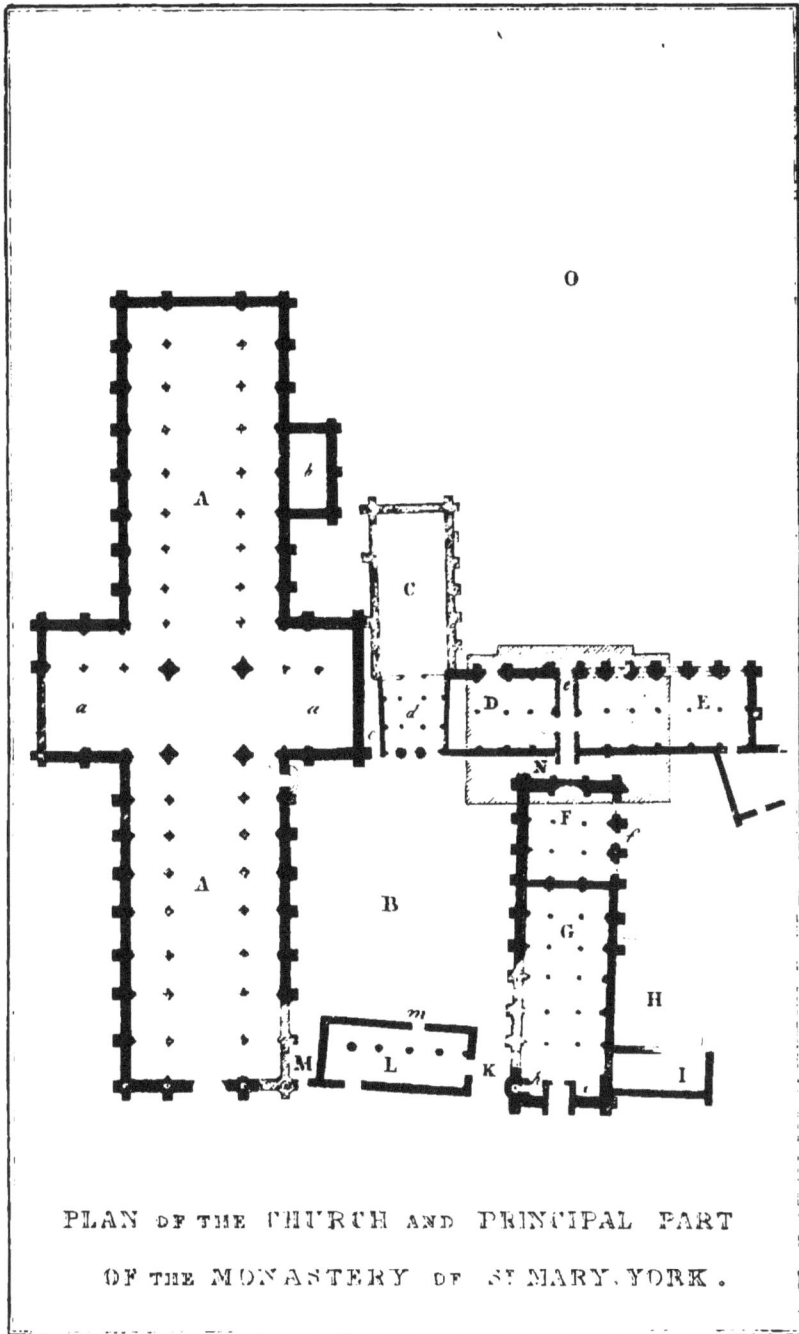

PLAN OF THE CHURCH AND PRINCIPAL PART
OF THE MONASTERY OF St MARY, YORK.

PREFACE.

A COMPARISON of this edition of the Hand-book to the York Museum, etc., with its immediate predecessors will show the great importance and variety of the additions that have been made during the last ten years. The Museum is now more worthy than it was of the ancient city which it illustrates, and of the great county of which that city is the capital. It is visited every year by strangers from all parts of the world, and the Council of the Yorkshire Philosophical Society appeal to all natives of the county to enable them to make the York Museum the best existing representation of what York and Yorkshire were in bygone days.

CONTENTS.

ADDENDA ET CORRIGENDA.

———

P. 55. Under the coffin of Theodorianus, and helping to support it, is a portion of a rude and almost defaced Roman inscription, which can only be detected in a peculiar light. Parts of three lines of letters may be traced. The middle line begins with the letters CIVI.

P. 98. *a.* The figure, here supposed to be that of Atys, seems to hold an apple in his hand, and Dr. Hübner suggests that Paris is represented, and that he is holding out the meed of beauty.

I.

ANTIQUITIES IN THE GROUNDS OF THE YORKSHIRE PHILOSOPHICAL SOCIETY.

THE grounds in which the Museum of the Yorkshire Philosophical Society stands occupy above one-half of the ancient Close of the Benedictine Abbey of St. Mary; with a small portion of the moat of the city wall, and of the enclosure within which the Hospital of St. Leonard formerly stood.

The Visitor, upon his first entrance into these grounds, will observe, on his right hand, the remains of the ancient Hospital of St. Leonard ; but he is advised to pass over these for the present, and to direct his attention, first of all, to the remains of a much older date immediately adjoining those of the Hospital, a portion of THE FORTIFICATIONS OF THE ROMAN STATION OF EBURACUM, the capital of Roman Britain ; erected, it is probable, toward the close of the first century of the Christian era. These remains, consisting of a part of the wall and an angle-tower, are in a remarkably good state of preservation, considering their great age, and the dangers to which they have been exposed amidst the various vicissitudes which the city of York has experienced, during the long and often much troubled period that has elapsed since Britain was abandoned by the Romans. The exterior of the angle-tower has suffered most, but the original work, which remains unchanged, may at once be distinguished from ·the rude repairs it has received in later times, and from the portion raised upon it, when it was made a part of the wall of York in mediæval times.

B

The masonry of the exterior surface of the Roman wall, and of the whole breadth of the wall of the tower, consists of regular courses of small ashlar stones, with a string of large Roman tiles, five in depth, inserted between the nineteenth and twentieth courses of the stones from the foundation. Turning by the tower to the right hand, and passing through a doorway in the present city wall joining the tower, the visitor will come upon another portion of the Roman wall connected with the angle-tower and proceeding from it in a north-easterly direction, at nearly a right angle. This has been traced, as far as the city gate called Bootham Bar, where the foundations, and some interesting fragments of the old Roman gate were discovered. Several of these fragments are in the Museum. In 1876, some farther remains of the gate were found, with a large portion of a pillar, showing that the structure was somewhat similar to the arch of Severus at Rome. Between the angle-tower and this gate, portions of two wall towers, and one entire small chamber, have been found buried with the wall in the modern rampart.* These towers and the wall immediately connected with them were removed, with the exception of a small portion in the garden of the last house in St. Leonard's Place, when that entrance into the city was formed.

The masonry of the interior of the angle-tower, reaching very nearly, it is probable, to its original height, is remarkably fresh and perfect, owing to its having been concealed during many ages by an accumulation of soil which was removed soon after the building came into the possession of the Society, in 1831. The tower has been divided by a wall, a small part of which is still remaining, into two equal portions. At the height of about five feet there seems to have been originally a timber floor; and above this, at the height of

* See " Eburacum, or York under the Romans," p. 52.

about nine feet, another floor. The lower compartments had a mortar floor laid upon sand; and having no light but from the entrances, may have been used as depositories for stores or arms. The two apartments above these were probably guard-rooms; each of them having a narrow window or aperture, so placed as to enable those within to observe what was passing without, along the line of each wall. The opening of these apertures externally was not more than six inches in width; but within, it expanded to about five feet; their height, owing to the change that has been made in the upper part of

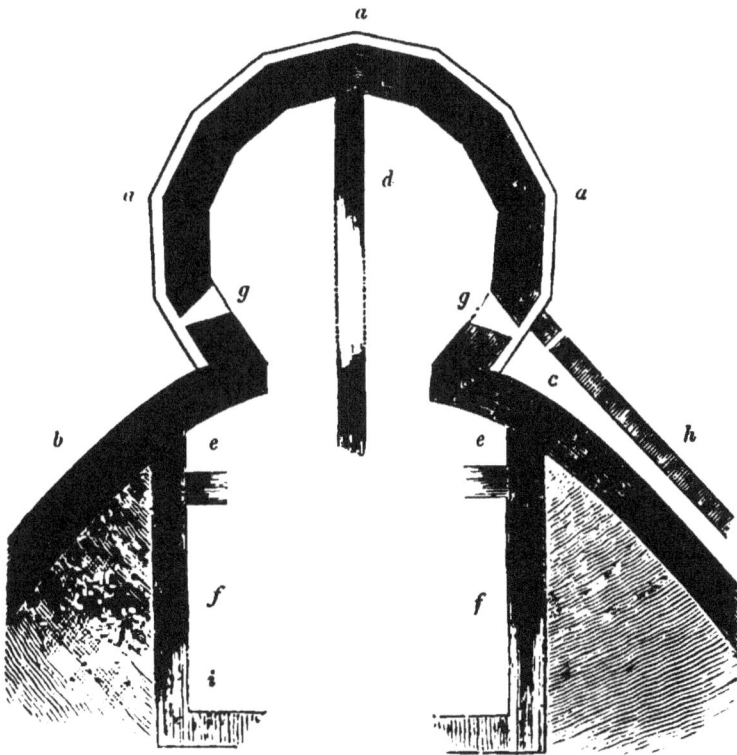

the tower, cannot be exactly ascertained. The annexed wood-cut will exhibit a clear view of the arrangement of this part of the ancient fortification. The diameter of the interior at the base or floor, is about 33 feet 6 inches : the plan consists of ten sides of a nearly regular thirteen-sided figure, forming nine very obtuse angles : whence it has obtained the name of THE MULTANGULAR TOWER.

a. a. a. The multangular wall of the tower.

b. The wall of the Roman station proceeding from the tower in the direction of Lendal and Coney-street.

c. The wall proceeding in the direction of Bootham Bar.

d. The wall dividing the tower into two portions.

e. e. The wall at the entrance into the tower. Traces of another similar wall have been seen at *i*.

f. f. Walls built for the purpose of supporting the interior ramparts.

g. g. The apertures in the upper rooms of the tower, which commanded a view of the exterior of the walls.

h. The modern city wall.

The stone coffins deposited in the tower were found in different Roman burial places in the immediate neighbourhood of York. They are rudely formed of a coarse grit stone, and are without inscriptions. In that which is marked by the letters H. F., discovered in 1831 in Heslington field, about a mile from York, were some few remains of a female which had been covered with plaster (gypsum) in a liquid state. This plaster, exhibiting a cast of the body, together with some trinkets imbedded in it, may be seen in the upper room of the Hospitium, in the case marked I.

The multangular tower with the wall adjoining it is the chief portion of the fortifications of Eburacum or Roman York, existing above ground. But in excavating for sewers and other purposes, various portions of the foundations of such fortifications have been found ; by means of which the exact extent of one side, and the direction of the other sides of the

Roman Station have been ascertained with tolerable accuracy. The East side runs from Market Street to the Multangular Tower in the Museum Gardens; the North from this tower, along the line of the City Wall, to the corner of Gillygate and Lord Mayor's Walk; the West, follows the City Wall through Mr. Gray's garden (where it was discovered in 1861) past Monk Bar, (where a considerable portion of it may be seen in the inner rampart,) to a point not very far distant, near the site of the old church of St. Helen on the Walls. As to the shape of the South side there is some doubt. By drawing a straight line from the site of St. Helen's Church to Market Street, the wall would pass through Church Street and Parliament Street, but a portion of the wall recently discovered in Aldwark crossed that street at so sharp an angle that if the line were carried out the greater part of the Shambles and Parliament Street would be brought within the limits of the camp. It may be that want of space obliged the Romans to break up the earlier arrangement of the walls, and to take in more room, thus destroying the original square. It appears, however, that Roman York occupied a comparatively small portion of the site of modern York, and that it was entirely on the north side of the River Ouse; the south side being occupied, as recent discoveries have shewn, by extensive baths, temples, villas, and places of burial, on the road leading from Eburacum to Calcaria (Tadcaster), the next station towards the south. It has been hitherto conjectured that the Roman Station of Eburacum was of a rectangular form, of about 536 yards, by about 470; having four principal gates or entrances; four principal angle-towers; and a series of minor towers, or turrets, from twenty-five to thirty in number. It is more probable, I think, that the camp was five-sided, and had a larger area.

The first of the plates facing the title-page represents what was considered to be the position and extent of Eburacum, and the situation and extent of the modern city, within the limits of its walls.

From the interior of the Multangular Tower, the visitor may pass to the remains of a religious establishment, next in point of antiquity to those of the Roman Station; and forming a part of THE HOSPITAL OF ST. LEONARD. The foundation of this religious house is ascribed to the Anglo-Saxon King Athelstan; who, returning from a successful expedition against the Scots, in the year 936, and finding in the Cathedral church of York some poor religious persons, called Colidei or Culdees, devoting themselves to works of charity and piety, granted them a piece of ground near the Cathedral, on which they might erect a Hospital; adding, for the support of it, one thrave of corn out of every carucate of land in the bishoprick of York. William the Conqueror confirmed this grant. William Rufus enlarged the site of their Hospital, and built for them a Church, which was dedicated, as the Hospital had been, to St. Peter. Henry I. still farther enlarged the Close of the establishment, extending it to the banks of the river; confirming their privileges, and granting them additional lands. Stephen re-built the Hospital, and dedicated it to St. Leonard, and henceforth it was, probably, independent of the Minster. All its privileges and possessions were confirmed and enlarged by successive kings, and additional grants were made from time to time by the wealthy and devout, so that it became one of the largest and best endowed foundations of the kind in the North of England. Mr. Drake, in his History of York, says that the number of persons constantly maintained in this Hospital, besides those relieved elsewhere from its funds, was 90; including a master or warden, 13 brethren, 8 sisters, 4 secular priests, 30 choristers, 2 school-masters, 26 bedemen, and 6 servitors. The Hospital was surrendered in the year 1539, at the dissolution of religious houses, when the clear yearly rental was stated to be £362 11s. 10¼d., equal, it is probable, to £5000 at the present time.

Of the first portion of the remains of this large establishment which presents itself to the notice of the visitor, immediately upon leaving the Multangular Tower, no satisfactory account can be given. It consists merely of the bases of four pillars, small portions of two shafts, and one capital, evidently parts of two rows of pillars of very unequal dimensions, ranged parallel to the Roman wall. It is highly probable that there are the remains of corresponding pillars in the ground not occupied by the Society; and that the ground plan of the structure to which they belonged may be truly represented by the annexed wood-cut: *a. a. a. a.* denoting the bases now seen.

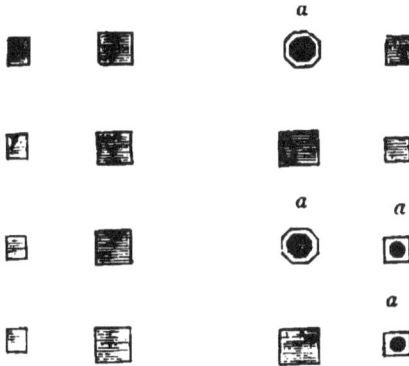

If this be correct, this part of the building consisted of three compartments, separated by rows of pillars. But of the character of the superstructure, and the purpose of the building, it is in vain to form any conjecture.

Leaving these, the visitor will proceed to the more interesting remains of what in all probability were the Ambulatory and Chapel of the Infirmary of St. Leonard's Hospital, which was leased to the Society by the Corporation in 1841. The covered cloister or Ambulatory appears to have consisted of five, or perhaps six aisles, in two of which was a large fire-place ; for the benefit, no doubt, of the infirm and sickly, for whose use the Ambulatory was designed. The exterior aisle, on the side towards the Multangular Tower, was most probably inclosed by a wall. Above the Ambulatory were the chambers or wards of the infirmary ; adjoining to which is the beautiful, small chapel, opening to the chamber, so that the sick persons who were confined to their beds, might have the comfort of hearing the celebration of the divine offices. The eastern end of the chapel indicates the period of its erection ; the style of the architecture being that of the early part of the 13th century, and it is no doubt the work of John Romanus, Treasurer of the Minster, and the builder of the North Transept, who is said to have restored the Hospital of St. Leonard. The Ambulatory belongs to rather an earlier age. How access was obtained to the chamber and the chapel, does not clearly appear ; there being no remains of a staircase. Adjoining the Ambulatory is the ancient entrance into the Hospital from the river ; on the banks of which was a staith or wharf, appropriated to the Hospital, called St. Leonard's landing.

On the left hand, as you go beneath the arch, is a large stone coffin, boldly cut, with a label for an inscription which has never been put on it. The label ends with *peltæ*, resembling the letter E. This coffin was found in 1874, near the Scarbro' Railway Bridge, lying north and south, and immediately in front of it, a skeleton (probably that of some servant of the deceased) was discovered, buried 'bolt upright.' The two sarcophagi next to this are a pair, and were found in the year 1813, in Clifton, at a place called One Tree Hill, in the grounds of Mr. David Russell (now the property of Mr. Thomlinson-Walker.) There are some slight traces on these coffins of effaced inscriptions, showing that they have been used at least twice. These were deposited here by the Dean and Chapter in 1862.* The fourth sarcophagus on the same side is carefully finished for an inscription, but one of the corners has been damaged, and on that account the tomb was probably bought cheap out of a Roman stonemason's yard. *On the right side* is another large coffin which has probably been used more than once, as there are some traces of a defaced label and inscription. The only letters remaining are the usual D. M. upon the lid. This was found in the New Railway Station in 1873. Near this coffin are two side stones of a Roman well, discovered in Tanner Row, at the end of Barker Lane. A large British coffin is near, hollowed out of a single oak tree, and containing, when discovered, several skeletons. It was found near Sunderlandwick, in the East Riding, and was presented by Mr. E. H. Reynard in 1856. Appended to the wall as you enter the archway, on the right hand, is an inscription recording the building of the Market Cross in Pavement in 1671-2, by Marmaduke Rawdon. † The cross was removed in 1813, and this inscription was presented to the Museum in 1835 by Mr. J. Smith. On the stone is the following additional record, placed immediately below the arms of the city :--" *The above inscription, part of the Market Cross taken down in* 1813, *was restored and placed here with the sanction of the Yorkshire Philosophical Society by W. F. Rawdon, M.D.*" The hand of the restorer is again needed.

Outside, with their heads towards the street, are six stone coffins, very coarsely wrought, discovered during the excavations in 1872-3.

---

* These are figured in Mr. Wellbeloved's Eboracum, p. 104, and Wright's Celt, Roman, and Saxon, and are a good sample of these ponderous sarcophagi which have been found in great numbers around York. There are between thirty and forty of them in the grounds of the Society.

† The inscription may be found in Drake's Eboracum; and in the preface to Mr. Davies' Life of Marmaduke Rawdon p 39.

B 2

Adjoining to this entrance, on the site of the present street, there was another aisle, the use of which is not known. The staircase leading to the Infirmary and the Chapel may have been at the northern end of it. Of the use to which the room under the Chapel was applied, no satisfactory account can be given.

The huge Roman tomb, composed of ten large slabs of grit stone, deposited in this room, marked I., was discovered in the year 1848, not far from the entrance to the North Eastern Railway Station, through the ramparts of the city wall. It contained the remains of a body which had been placed in a coffin of cedar, and covered with gypsum. The coffin had entirely perished, with the exception of a few very small fragments: but the gypsum remained, exhibiting a cast of the body over which it had been poured. This cast is deposited in the upper room of the Hospitium, in the case marked Q. b.

The Roman coffin marked II., was discovered in July, 1851, about three feet below the surface, near Skeldergate Postern, by the side of the road leading to Bishopthorpe. It contained a cast of the bodies of a female and a child, deposited in the upper room of the Hospitium, in the case marked E.

The Roman coffin marked III., was found in the garden of the late Mr. John Prest, without Micklegate Bar. It contained a few bones, and a jet ring.—*Mr. J. W. Graves.*

The coffin marked IV., was found at the Mount.—*Mr. W. Driffield.*

In the Larger Vaulted Room are some Mediæval remains. (*a*) A portion of the stone figure of St. Leonard, the patron of the Hospital. (*b*) Many of the stones of an arch found in the excavation for St. Leonard's Place, and a part, no doubt, of the ancient Hospital. (*c*) Part of a sepulchral slab removed from Christ-Church when it was restored. It probably commemorates John Towthorp, butcher, and Margery his wife, who were buried there in the 15th century.

Returning by the Multangular Tower, the visitor passes again over what was formerly the moat of the city wall, and enters on the precincts of the ABBEY OF ST. MARY.

The original foundation of this once large and opulent establishment ascends to a period prior to the Norman Conquest. About the year 1050, Siward, a noble Dane, and Earl of Northumberland, began to erect a minster or church here, which he dedicated to St. Olave, and in which he is said to have been buried. Six years after the Conquest, three zealous monks, Aldwine, Elfwine, and Reinfrid, from the Abbey of Evesham, came into the North with the view of reviving monastic life there, almost extinct through the long continued violence of the Danish invaders. Having been very successful in their mission on the banks of the Tyne, Reinfrid came southwards to Streaneshalh (Whitby), where still remained the ruins of a Saxon convent founded by St. Hilda. Here he was allowed by Earl Perci, to whom this fee belonged, to build a Priory and was soon joined by several who had devoted themselves to a monastic life. Among these was one named Stephen, to whom the government of the priory was committed. But having made himself obnoxious to the Earl, he was driven from the priory, and retired to Lastingham on the eastern moors, where a religious house had been established in the Saxon times. This he refounded, but was shortly driven thence also by his powerful adversary. Under the protection of Alan of Brittany, Earl of Richmond, to whom the Church of St. Olave founded by Siward belonged, Stephen, in the year 1087, came to York; and having received from his new patron the grant of the Church, and of four acres of land adjoining it, he proceeded, with the approbation and aid of the king, to convert it into a monastery. Eleven years afterwards,

William Rufus enlarged the grant of Alan, and laid the foundation of a new and larger church which he dedicated to the Blessed Virgin Mary. There is evidence in what yet remains of the entrance to the Chapter House, and in many of the carved fragments which have been disinterred, that the buildings of the monastery were not completed prior to the reign of Stephen : perhaps not so early. Gervase of Canterbury records the burning of the Minster and Abbey during that reign : but if either of these buildings suffered from fire at that time, the injury, it is probable, was of no great extent. Nearly 200 years after its first foundation by the second William, the celebrated Abbat, Simon de Warwick, who governed the Abbey between the years 1259 and 1299, laid the foundation of a new large choir in 1271, and lived to see it completed. The rebuilding of the other portions of the Church followed, no doubt ; but few records remain to inform us by whom the work was carried on. In 1278 Archbishop Giffard granted an indulgence to those who contributed to the building of the tower. This was struck by lightning in 1376 and was burned to the ground. It was surmounted, probably, by a spire of wood, covered with lead. Simon de Warwick is said also to have built, in 1266, the wall and towers surrounding the Close of the Abbey; the rampart of earth, by which it had been previously enclosed, not being sufficient to protect it from the hostile attacks of the citizens, between whom and the monks frequent quarrels are recorded to have arisen. It may also have been found necessary to have a better defence against the incursions of the Scots. In the year 1540, the Monastery of St. Mary shared the fate of other monastic houses, and was surrendered to the King by William Dent, the last Abbat ; the clear annual rental at that time being £1650 0s. 7¼d. At the dissolution there were 50 Monks in the establishment, including the Abbat, the Prior, and Sub-Prior; to whom may be added 150 servants; supposing them to bear the same proportion to the number of Monks and the dignity of the Abbat as we find in other religious houses.

The Abbat of St. Mary's enjoyed the dignity of the mitre, and was summoned to parliament. The Mitred Abbeys, at the Dissolution were for the most part granted by the king to noble or wealthy families, in consideration of past services, of exchange of lands, or of the payment of a sum of money. The Monastery of St. Mary was retained by the Crown.

The Churches of some of the greater Monasteries were at the Dissolution converted into Episcopal Churches; but York had its Cathedral long before the foundation of the Abbey of St. Mary; and the neighbouring parish of St. Olave possessed a church fully adequate to its wants, adjoining the Abbey, on the site, it is probable, of Earl Siward's church. The Abbey church therefore was doomed to destruction: and the monastic buildings were partially destroyed, to provide a site and materials for a royal palace. The site chosen adjoined the south transept of the church, the buildings of the Monastery extending from the transept nearly to the wall of the Abbey Close; including the Chapter house with its vestibule, the Library, the Scriptorium, and several other rooms.

About the close of the year 1822, the Yorkshire Philosophical Society was founded; and in the year 1827 it obtained a grant from the Crown of nearly three acres of ground within the ancient precincts of the Monastery, including the remains of the Abbey church, with the exception of the choir, as a site for buildings appropriated to the purposes of science.* The spot selected by the society

* In 1836, the Society was enabled, by the liberal bequest of Dr. Beckwith, to purchase from the Crown all that part of the Manor Shore which lay between the Waterworks and Marygate, and between the Museum garden and the Ouse.

happened to be that on which a Royal Palace appears to have been erected after the Dissolution; a small portion of which, a wall with a large fire-place, was still remaining; forming the boundary, in that part, of the ground granted to the society.* From the appearance of the surface it was conjectured that the ground would be found full of the ruins of the later, if not of the more ancient structure, perhaps of both edifices; but the first opening of the ground discovered, not mere heaps of mutilated stones, but considerable portions of the lower apartments of the Monastery, of spacious and elegant door-ways, of octagonal columns rising to the height of five or six feet, standing as they had stood before the dissolution of the Abbey, intersected by the foundations of the Palace; while in the intervening spaces were scattered numerous fragments consisting of richly carved capitals, mouldings, and elegant tracery work. Of similar remains, much of which appeared to have belonged to the once large and magnificent chapter-house, the foundation walls of the palace, when broken up, were found to consist. The octagonal pillars, removed only a few inches from their original position, may be seen in one of the lower rooms of the Museum, under the Zoological Room; the most interesting of the sculptured remains are deposited in the Hospitium. These discoveries led to farther excavations; nearly every part of the ground granted to the Society was explored; and although the result was not so satisfactory as could have been desired, nothing more than the bases or the rough foundations of pillars, and the mere rudiments of walls in many places being traced, yet the situation and extent of the principal portions of this splendid monastic establishment were ascertained; and thus the ichnography of another great Abbey was obtained, for

* See the plate at page 574 of Drake's Eboracum, and the Report of Communications to the Monthly Meetings for 1858 p. 21.

the gratification and instruction of those to whom the economy of monastic structures is an interesting subject of inquiry.

By means of the plate already given, the visitor, it is hoped, will be enabled to form some idea of the arrangement and situation of the buildings which formed the Abbey. The shaded part shows the position of the Museum.

AA. The Church of the Monastery, remarkable for the great length of the choir, the site of which was not included in the government grant to the society.* About half way from the western entrance to the central tower, between the fifth and sixth windows of the nave, the floor of the church appears to have been raised by one step, about seven inches in height : the floor of the tower and the transepts appears also to have had a farther elevation of about seventeen inches, to which there must have been an ascent of three steps between the western pillars of the tower and the last intercolumniations of the nave.

a a. The Transepts. *b.* A vestry ; or a side chapel.

The nave and choir had two side-aisles ; the transepts had only one aisle, on the eastern side.

There was only one entrance to the nave at the western end ; on the northern side was another doorway, the beautiful mouldings of which can be seen only from the adjoining church yard : on the southern side, near the transept, was an entrance from the quadrangle, and probably there was another near the western end, from the dormitory.

The remains of semicircular processes or apses, towards the east, appear in the north transept ; and similar remains were discovered, when the eastern side of the north transept was excavated. In these, no doubt, were the windows of the

* By an arrangement with the Governors of the Wilberforce School for the Blind, it is now included in the grounds of the Society (1869). The Society also acquired in 1879 an acre of ground to the north of the chancel of the Abbey, a portion of the old Bowling-green of the King's Manor.

transepts on that side. An apsis of much larger dimensions, a few feet within the site of the choir, has since been observed, which appears to have been the eastern termination of the church built by the Abbat Stephen.

It appears that in the rebuilding of the church by Abbat Simon, many portions of the old fabric of coarse grit stone were suffered to remain, being encased by the new work of limestone. This may be seen in the remaining pier or buttress, in the north-east corner of the north transept: and yet more extensively in the south transept.

B. The great Quadrangle; in its usual situation, on the south side of the nave. It had, probably, a pent-house cloister, on every side. The level of the quadrangle near the transept was 3 feet 9 inches below the level of the church, the entrance to which, by the door before mentioned, was consequently by steps, one of which may now be seen.

c. A narrow passage from the quadrangle leading to the space between the Choir and the Chapter House: perhaps to the vestry and the Abbat's residence.

c. The Chapter House. Of this important part of the monastery nothing remains but the lowest portions of the foundations of grit stone. All above this seems to have been removed to make room for the Palace, and the spacious cellars, the walls of which, still remaining entire in the grounds belonging to the School for the Blind, contain many of the finely sculptured stones that once adorned the entrance and the interior of this large and magnificent apartment. The approach to the Chapter House from the quadrangle was through a beautiful vestibule (d), supported by two rows of pillars forming three aisles. The richly sculptured piers, part of the portal of the Chapter House, one of which, nearly perfect, remains, are said to have been crowned by the beautiful arch which is preserved in the Hospitium, but this is a matter of doubt.

D. An apartment divided into three parts by three octagonal pillars, from which the vaulting sprung. These pillars are still standing in the lower apartments of the Museum; but not exactly in their original situation. To what use this room in the monastery was appropriated cannot be ascertained. If there were no apartments above it, (which however, is not very probable), it may have been the Library or Scriptorium, or both. The principal entrance was from the passage (e). It had also an entrance from the Abbat's Court.

E. Another apartment of a similar character, 78 feet in length; the use of which is also unknown. The entrance was from the passage. It was connected also with another of the monastic buildings at its south-east corner, which was, probably, the Infirmary.

F. An apartment which, if all the finely worked bosses found buried in it had originally adorned its vaultings, must have been a splendid room. It had a large ornamented fire-place, guarded by a stone fender. The level of the floor was from two to three feet below that of the quadrangle to which it adjoined, and the entrance was at (f), from a court on the south side. The room was divided into three equal parts by elegant moulded pillars, and furnished with a stone seat on every side. This is thought to have been the parlour; or perhaps the "common house," which is described as being usually on the right hand on going out of the cloisters to the Infirmary, and as "having a fire constantly by day in winter for the use of the monks who were allowed no other fire.* The fire-place is still remaining as it was found, in the lower part of the Museum, beneath the Hall. The beautiful bosses or ceiling knots found in this room, seem to have been most

* See Fosbroke's British Monachism, p. 69.

carefully preserved by the builders of the palace, as if they had foreseen their future exhumation by those who would appreciate them more justly than they did, who doomed this once splendid apartment to destruction. Several of these bosses may now be seen, among other beautiful remains of the monastery, in the lower room of the Hospitium.

G. The site of the Refectory, 82 feet long, and 37 feet wide. This room was longitudinally divided into three parts by two rows of octangular pillars, five in each row, and separated from the apartment F by a wall only 12 in. thick. The entrance was not, as usual, from the quadrangle, but from the western end, by a large double doorway. On the left of the entrance at (h), were found the lower steps of a spacious stone staircase, leading perhaps to the dormitory. A recess at (i), just within the apartment, had a pavement of plain glazed tiles, 9 in. square, purple and yellow alternately.

H. The great Kitchen of the Abbey.

I. A room adjoining to the kitchen, but not connected with it: perhaps the office of the Cellarer.

K. A passage from the quadrangle leading to the court in which was the entrance to the Refectory.

L. The Ambulatory or Cloister under the dormitory; very small when compared with that of Jervaux, or Kirkstall, and, especially, of Fountains. The dormitory may have extended over a part of the refectory. This cloister was on a lower level than that of the quadrangle, the access to which was by steps at (m). In this part of the quadrangle the monks held their school for the instruction of children sent to them from the neighbourhood; and two glazed tiles, on which was painted the alphabet in capital letters of the 15th century, to be read, with the exception of one line, from right to left, were found in the excavation of that part. The Lavatory at which the monks washed themselves, was probably on that side of the quadrangle; if not, it may have been, as at Worcester, on the western side of the ambulatory.

M. Apparently a passage between the ambulatory and the church: connecting, it is probable, a staircase from the dormitory with an entrance into the church near the western end of the nave. A passage of this kind may be observed at Fountains, Kirkstall, and other abbeys; and it was judiciously contrived, in order that the monks "might pass to their late or early devotions with the least possible exposure to the outer air."

N. The passage from the apartment F, from the Infirmary and other buildings of the monastery, and also from the abbat's residence, to the quadrangle, and thus to the Chapter House and the Church. Doors appear to have been placed at the entrance to the quadrangle, and at the end (*e*) of the passage from the abbat's court.

O. The site of the Abbat's House, which was called the King's Manor, and made the residence of the Lord Presidents of the North, the Royal Palace, built after the Dissolution, having been speedily dismantled. It appears to have undergone much alteration in the beginning of the reign of James I., who intended to make it his occasional residence; and afterwards in the reign of Charles I., under the direction of the Earl of Strafford. Nearly the whole of the King's Manor is now occupied by the Wilberforce School for the Blind.

Of other parts of the domestic buildings of the monastery the foundations were traced; but the remains were too small and imperfect to afford any indication of the purposes to which they had been appropriated.

Before the visitor leaves the church he should not fail to notice a striking peculiarity in the structure of the windows, the lights and tracery of which varied alternately in a very remarkable manner. The window nearest to the western front was divided by one mullion into two trefoil-headed lights, above which, in the head of the arch, was a six-foil light. The next window was divided by two mullions into three trefoil-headed lights, above which were placed three quatre-foil lights; and thus alternately along the whole of the nave.

Contemplating the Western front of the church, on his way to the Hospitium, which stands in the lower part of the grounds, and in which some of the most interesting fragments of the sculptured decorations of the abbey are deposited, the visitor will easily imagine how beautiful it must have been in its perfect state, crowned with turrets or spires, and crocketed pinnacles. The ornaments about the doorway must have been singularly elegant. In a deep hollow moulding between every column was figured the shoot of a vine, rising from the bottom, and at the top leaving its retreat, to pass in front of the head of the nearest column, so as to form a foliated capital. Nothing can be conceived more chaste or graceful.

On the right of the path leading to the Hospitium may be seen the arch of the gateway, which formed the principal entrance to the monastery. The arch and arcade belong to the Norman period; but the building attached to them, a part only of the gatehouse, the portion above the archway on the other side of it being destroyed, is evidently of a later date. The porter resided in the gatehouse. The lower part of the portion still standing appears to have been the prison of the abbey, in which debtors to the abbat, in the extensive liberty of St. Mary, and perhaps others subject to his power, were confined.* The upper part was probably the room in which the abbat held courts. This building, and that which corresponded to it on the other side of the archway, in which was a

* The abbat of St. Mary had a gallows, not far from the site of the mill in Burton-stone Lane.

chapel dedicated to the Virgin, called "The chapel of our Lady at the gate," must have been added to the ancient gate, in the latter half of the fifteenth century.*

By the side of the walk at the north end of the Hospitium, are two stones, one of which was discovered near the gateway, at a considerable depth. They are, probably, *cippi*, which often marked Roman graves. During the Railway excavations of 1872-3 some stones which no doubt served this purpose, resembling these somewhat in shape, were discovered. They are now laid against the south wall of the Hospitium within the archway.

Opposite to these *cippi*, are two stone coffins, placed in the position in which they were found under the new Station Hotel in 1874. One contained the bones of a lady, under whose head a single jet hair-pin was found. By the side of this coffin, with the head resting against the foot, was a skeleton, under the back of which were the remains of a wooden box, containing six glass vessels and several ornaments. These, which were unhappily much broken, may be seen in CASE C, upstairs. In the other coffin were the bones of two young girls. At the head of this coffin, two food dishes of coarse pottery, and two drinking vessels of glass, were found, intended no doubt for the use of the departed. These are also preserved in CASE N, upstairs.

Beneath the staircase to the upper room was preserved for a long time the portcullis, which formerly did service at Micklegate Bar. This has been removed to the Museum for protection.

There is no documentary or traditionary evidence respecting either the age of the building now called the HOSPITIUM or the uses to which it was applied. It is conjectured that it had been erected for the entertainment of those strangers who

---

* There is an account of this chapel in the Transactions for 1879.

were not admitted to the principal apartments of the monastery; the lower room having been the refectory, and the upper, originally of the same extent, the dormitory. The position of this building, near one of the entrances to the monastery, and the correspondence of the plan of the lower room with that of the refectory for the monks, tend to confirm that conjecture. The portion of the lower apartment on the left of the doorway, lighted by five narrow windows, was originally separated by a cross wall from the other portion, forming perhaps a store-room or buttery.

If this building was originally constructed partly of stone and partly of timber and plaster, it must have been one of the later structures belonging to the monastery. Yet it cannot have been the latest; for the manner in which the adjoining archway is attached to it, indicates that this archway was subsequently erected. And this is evidently of the same age as the building adjoining the ancient abbey-gate. This archway appears to have been the entrance into the interior of the abbey-close from the river, and may be termed the Watergate. Between it and the river was a wall, built by abbat Thomas de Malton, in 1334, which was standing in a dilapidated condition when Drake published his Eboracum, as may be seen in the plate, at page 331 of that work. The apartments attached to this gateway may have been the residence not only of the gate-keeper, but also of those whose duty it was to attend to the strangers who were received into the Hospitium.

On the sides of the door as you enter the Hospitium are the basin of a Roman well and a squared gritstone found in Micklegate in 1853, near St. Martin's Church. This is probably one of the basement stones of a Temple on which a column has rested.

Seal of the Abbey of St. Mary's, York, from a cast taken from a seal among the Records of the Duchy of Lancaster. *

II.
ANTIQUITIES CHIEFLY IN THE
LOWER APARTMENT OF THE HOSPITIUM.

The Antiquities in this apartment belong to the Roman, the Anglo-Saxon, the Anglo-Norman, and the Mediæval periods. With very few exceptions, they have all been found in York, or the immediate neighbourhood: the Mediæval are chiefly remains of the Abbey.

1. Roman.

The first object of attention in this apartment is a Roman Tessellated Pavement, fourteen feet three inches square.

* See Proceedings of Y. P. S., May 4, 1858, for notice of an alleged seal of St. Mary's Abbey. A better impression of the seal represented above is preserved among the deeds of the Company of Merchant Adventurers, York.

When perfect, the pattern was composed chiefly of the common labyrinthine fret, and five heads; one in the centre, representing the head of Medusa, which has been too much injured to admit of reparation; and four symbolical representations of the Seasons. The head nearest the entrance, representing Autumn with a bunch of grapes, having been much injured, partly in the removal and partly by two inundations of the river, has been repaired with modern materials; the next head nearer to the window, with a bird on the shoulder, represents Spring; the third, with a dead branch, Winter; and the fourth, with a rake, Summer. The whole pavement was taken up and relaid at a higher level in the year 1868.

This pavement was discovered in the year of 1853, in Toft Green, near Micklegate Bar, about fourteen feet below the present surface, with portions of another, and the border of a third now in the possession of the Society. Immediately beneath it were found an empty urn, covered with a square tile; a coin, first-brass, of Hadrian; and a third-brass coin of Claudius Gothicus, with the legend *Divo Claudio* on the obverse; proving that this pavement was not laid down before A.D. 270, the year in which Claudius died. About twelve or fourteen inches below this pavement, a floor composed of cement was found on which were scattered many tessellæ, finished and unfinished, and a piece of iron conjectured to be a tool used in shaping them.—*The Corporation of York*, 1853.

The raised Platform, at the upper end of the room, is formed chiefly of red sandstone, which is seen in abundance at Aldborough, and out of which the floor of one of the Roman baths, which were discovered in 1839, was composed. On this many of the inscribed stones are placed.

The order pursued in this list is much the same as that adopted by Dr. Hübner in his Roman Inscriptions of Britain.

A classification of the sculptured stones has been attempted, precedence being given to the divinities. It has been thought advisable also to give notices of the Roman sculptures found in York, which are either in other museums, or are lost. The inscriptions are given in ordinary type, and no notice is taken of peculiar lettering, owing to the difficulty in representing it.

No. 1. The greater part of a figure with a fragmentary inscription beneath its feet, 24 in. high, by 13 in width.

The inscription is as follows :—

D VOL. IRE . . . .

ARIMANIV. . . .

the remainder of the label having been broken off. Professor Hübner proposes to restore this, and to read *Deo Ævo, Volusii, Irenæus et Arimanius, posuerunt.* Thus the name Volusius is common to two brothers, Irenæus and Arimanius.

The figure is supposed to represent Time, Æon or Ævum. The head, which is missing, is believed to have been that of a lion, as symbolizing strength. The so-called belt around the waist, is probably a snake representing eternity. The right hand holds a rod, with which time was measured ; the left a bunch of keys reminding us of the opening and closing of all things. There is in the Museum at Bonn the upper part of a figure showing the lion's head and the measuring rod.* This remarkable sculpture was found under the City Wall, near the New Railway Station, in June, 1874, and is placed in the Entrance Hall of the Museum.—*The Directors N.E. Railway Company,* 1874.

---

* *cf.* Dr. Hübner's Paper in the Transactions of the Archæological Society at Bonn, pp. 149—154, where the York stone is engraved. *cf.* also the Transactions of the York Philosophical Society for 1877.

C

No. 2. A small altar, 2 feet by 1, with letters elegantly
cut, found in 1846 in the rubble foundation under one of the
pillars of the church of St. Denis, in York. It is inscribed :

DEO

A R C I A C O N

ET N. AVGSI

MAT. VITALIS

ORD. V. S. L. M.

This inscription, which can be properly represented only by
an engraving,* has been variously interpreted. In the previous
editions of the Catalogue, it has been read *Deo Arciacon et
Numini Augusti Simatius Vitalis Ordovix Votum Solvit Libens
Merito*, Ordovix being interpreted as one of the Ordovices, a
tribe which inhabited the northern part of Wales.

The latter part of the reading of Dr. Hübner is to be
preferred : *Deo Arciaconi † et Numini Augusti Maternius (?)
Vitalis. Ordo*, etc,, the word *Ordo* being equivalent to *Cen-
turio.—Purchased*, 1848.

** A base or pedestal of grit stone, 2 feet 10 inches broad, on
which a statue had rested. It bore the following inscription :

BRITANNIÆ

SANCTÆ

P. NIKOMEDES

AVGG. NN.

LIBERTVS.

Showing that it was a votive statue to the genius of Britain,
set up by Publius Nicomedes, a freedman of the Emperors,
probably Severus and Caracalla. This stone, which is now lost,
was found near Micklegate in 1740. There is a sketch of it
among the letters of Dr. Stukeley, which will shortly be edited
for the Surtees Society.

---

* Engraved in Journal Arch. Association, ii. 248, and in the Gloucester volume,
p. 151.

† It has been suggested that the name Arciacon may have been derived from
Artiaca, (Arcis-sur-Aube) in Gaul.

No. 3. An altar, 2ft. 3½in. by 1ft. 3½in., found in the Roman baths, when excavating the site of the old Railway Station, and inscribed :

DEAE
FORTVNAE
SOSIA
IVNCINA
Q. ANTONI
ISAVRICI
LEG. AVG.

From which it appears that it was dedicated to the goddess Fortune,* by Sosia Juncina, the wife of Quintus Antonius Isauricus, legate of the Emperor. Isauricus may have been legate of the province of Britain, or of the Sixth Legion. Dr. McCaul and Dr. Hübner prefer the latter.—*The Directors of the North Eastern Railway*, 1889.

No. 4. A portion of a base or pedestal on which a figure of Fortune has stood, the feet of which still remain. It is 7in. high and 3½in. broad. Part of the statue itself, 7in. high, was found with it, but is not in the museum. The letters are rudely cut, and are as follows, the right side of the stone being wanting. This stone is in the Entrance Hall of the Museum :

DAII. F(ORTVNAE)
PRO SA. P.
AVSPICA
MAIIS IM
I.D.D. LI
METROB
M.I. M.

This is probably part of a votive inscription to Fortune, for the safety of some one whose name has perished. *Dae Fortunae* is found on an altar at Bowes, and *ii* for *e* is a common substitution.† *Found near the Multangular Tower, which was cleared out in* 1831.

* This goddess was specially worshipped in connection with baths, and inscriptions have been found to her under the title of FORTUNA BALNEARIS.—*See Orelli Inscrr.* 5796—7. This altar is figured in Mr. Wellbeloved's Eburacum, p. 87.

† Wellbeloved, Eburacum, p. 96. The name of the dedicator may have been Metroblanus, which occurs in Grüter; or Metrobalus, a Dacian name.

No. 5. A small altar, 19in. high by 12in. wide, found under the New Railway Station, bearing the following inscription :

D. E. O.
GENIO
LO. CI
V. S. L. M.

The meaning is obvious. It is very rarely however that the words *Genio loci* have been found preceded by *Deo*. The Genius was a protecting spirit, or guardian angel of a person or place.—*The Directors of the North Eastern Railway*, 1875.

No. 6. A Votive tablet, 21in. long by 10in. in height, ascribed by Dr. Hübner to the first century. It was found in Coney Street, in 1702.

GENIO LOCI
FELICITER

Like the inscription which immediately follows, this stone was probably affixed to a Roman house, and expresses the wish that the Genius of the place may take charge of it.—*The Corporation of York*, 1838.

** A stone, 13in. long by 8in. high, found in 1814, when excavating for the new church at Norton, near Malton. The inscription is within a tablet or label, and is roughly cut :

FELICITER SIT
GENIO LOCI
SERVVLE. VTERE
FELIX TABERN
AM AVRIFI
CINAM.

It is a votive inscription to the Genius of the place, and was probably affixed to the goldsmith's house to which it alludes. There is a hint also to the slave, who had so much in his charge, to take due care of his master's property.—*Deposited by Mr. W. Walker, of Malton*, 1875.

No. 7. A marble tablet, 12½in. high by 7½in., representing a figure offering a libation to the local Genius, under the form

33

of a serpent coiled around an altar. It is said to have been found near the Roman wall in Northumberland. (In case J upstairs.)—*Rev. John Graham, of York*, 1823.

No. 8. A portion of a tablet, 21in. by 16½in., which records the restoration of a temple dedicated to Hercules. It was found at the corner of Ousegate and Nessgate in 1843, under the present Yorkshire Bank. The inscription runs:

HERCVL. . .
T. PERPET. .
AETER. . . .
EBVR . . . .
RES . . . . .

Dr. Hübner extends this, exempli gratia, merely: *Herculi Terentii Perpetuus et Aeternus (?) Eburacenses restituerunt.* It might also be *Titus Perpetuus Æternus Eburacensis restituit*, or the letter *T.* might stand for *Tarenti*, one of the titles of Hercules.*—*The Hargrove Collection*, 1847.

No. 9. A fragment of a small, nearly nude figure, 4in. high, without head or feet, wearing a rough cloak. It probably represented Hercules. Found near Micklegate Bar in 1854. (In Case J upstairs.)—*The Cook Collection*, 1872.

** An altar found on Bishophill in 1638, and presented in the following year to Charles I. It was afterwards in the house of the Fairfaxes, on Bishophill, and was given by the Duke of Buckingham, who married the heiress of that family, to the University of Oxford, where it now is.† The inscription, however, has disappeared, with the exception of the first three lines. It ran thus:

I. O. M.
DIS. DEABVSQVE
HOSPITALIBVS . PE
NATIBVSQ. OB CON
SERVATAM SALVTEM

* See Eburacum, Pref. p. vi.; and the Gloucester vol. Arch. Ass. p. 149.
† All the York Antiquarians believed that this altar was lost. It is engraved in the Marmora Oxoniensia.

SVAM. SVORVMQ
P. AEL. MARCIAN
VS . PRAEF. COH.
ARAM. SAC . F. NC. D

It is a thank offering to Jupiter, and all the friendly and household gods and goddesses, by Publius Ælius Marcianus, a prefect, for the preservation of the health of himself and his family. As to the interpretation of the last line there is considerable doubt.

No. 10. A small altar, 19in. by 10in., found in Mr. Bearpark's garden, the site of the present Fine Art Exhibition Building. There is a wreath on one side. Traces of letters in a bold character have been recently detected on it,* and the first line seems to contain the name

MARTI

Beyond this, and this is somewhat doubtful, it is impossible to go.

No. 11. An altar, 13in. high by 8in., of coarse sandstone, found in the garden of St. Mary's Convent, October, 1880. It is inscribed :

DEO MARTI. C
A G R I V S .
A R V S P E X .
V. S. L. M.

The names of the dedicator are found in inscriptions abroad. This is the first time that the word *Aruspex* has occurred in Britain. The two first letters in the word are ligulate.—*The Superioress of St. Mary's Convent, York*, 1881.

No. 12. A fine statue, probably representing the youthful Mars, found with the last-mentioned altar, and placed in a conspicuous position in the Entrance Hall of the Museum. It is carved in light coloured grit, probably by a local artist who has chosen as his model a marble statue. The figure, defective unfortunately in the feet and right arm, is 5ft. 10in. high, and

* By Mr. W. T. Watkin.

represents a martial personage in helmet, breastplate, and greaves, with the left hand resting upon a large oval shield. In the right hand, which has been in two parts, was, no doubt a lofty spear of wood or metal. The hair is arranged in fillets and the face is beautifully cut. This is the finest statue that has been found in Britain.*—*The Superioress of St. Mary's Convent*, 1881.

No. 13. An altar, 24in. high and 16in. in breadth, found in excavating for the North Eastern Railway, near the bridge in Holgate Lane. It has no inscription, but was probably dedicated to the *Deæ Matres*, or *Matronæ*, female deities, three in number, and supposed to have been introduced into Britain by the German auxiliaries. They are represented on the front of the altar, sitting in a recess. On the right side of the altar is a single male figure, and on the left two male figures.† On the fourth side, which is much defaced, there seems to have been the representation of an altar, and an animal, apparently a swine, standing before it.—*The Directors of the North Eastern Railway*, 1837.

No. 14. An altar, 2ft. 5in. high by 14in. wide, found at Doncaster (Danum) in 1781. It bears the following inscription :

MATRIBVS
M. NAN
TONIVS.
ORBIOTAL.
V. S. L. M.

On one side is cut a vase filled with flowers, on the other a pitcher. The inscription states that the altar was dedicated

* The figure may be compared with a much smaller one found at Housesteads, on the Roman wall, and figured in the Lapidarium Septentrionale, p. 121. It is probable that this too represents Mars to whom there are many altars inscribed in the same district.

† Such figures are of usual occurrence on these altars. See Mr. C. R. Smith's Roman London, p. 36. This altar is figured in Mr. Wellbeloved's Eburacum, p. 87.

to the Deæ Matres by M. Nantonius Orbiotalis.*—*Deposited by M. G. J. Jarratt*, 1856.

No. 15. A very pretty altar, 17in. high, which can only be represented by an engraving. The sides are fluted, as if made of reeds, and retain traces of colour, and the whole altar is richly ornamented.

C. IVLIVS
CRESCENS
MATRI
BVS DO
MESTICIS
V. S. M. L.

The name of the divinity is placed after that of the dedica-cator of the altar. He is styled Caius Julius Crescens, and may be perhaps identified with the Julius Crescens who dedi-cated au altar to Mercury at Birrens in Scotland. The *Matres Domesticæ* were the goddesses of the house and home and are commemorated in Britain by two altars, discovered in the neighbourhood of Carlisle. This altar was found in the garden of the Convent in Oct. 1880. *The Superioress of St. Mary's Convent*, 1881.

No. 16. A very. small altar, 10in. by 5½in., found in Micklegate in 1752, with several others which were uninscribed, and presented in 1785 to the Dean and Chapter of York.† It is now in the Entrance Hall of the Museum.

MAT. AF. ITA. GA.
M. MINV. MVDE
MIL. LEG. VI. VIC
GVBER. LEG. VI
V. S. L. L. M.

The inscription has been thus extended. *Matribus Afri-canis, Italicis, Gallicis, Marcus Minucius Mudenus, miles*

* There is an account of this altar in the Archæologia. vii. pp. 409 and 420, where the inscription is correctly read with the exception of the word *Orbiotalis*. It is engraved in Hunter's South Yorkshire, and C. R. Smith's Collectanea, iv. 53—4.

† *cf.* Smith's Collectanea, iv. 43—4.

legionis vi. victricis, gubernator legionis sextæ, votum solvit libens, lætus, merito. According to this reading Mudenus is regarded as the pilot of the Sixth Legion. Dr. Hübner conjectures that *guber.* is intended for *gubernatricibus*, assigning to the Deæ Matres the charge of the Sixth Legion. The only objection to this is the interpolation of the two preceding lines. On the other hand it must be said that it is extremely unlikely that the sculptor would mention the legion in two contiguous lines in connection with the same person.—*Deposited by the Dean and Chapter*, 1862.

No. 17. An imperfect altar, 8½in. by 7in., with very rude letters, found in 1850, in Park Place, Monkgate. The two first letters are missing :

MATRIBVS
SVIS. MARCVS
RVSTIVS. V. S. L.
MASSA. L. M.

The name of the dedicator is Marcus Rustius Massa, but, instead of placing these names in a continuous line, the engraver breaks off after *Rustius, Massa,* in the line below, filling up the vacant space with the votive formula. *Matribus suis,* means the *Deæ Matres* of the dedicator's own country.— *Mr. Wm. Thompson*, 1871.

No. 18. The upper part of a rudely sculptured stone, discovered many years ago in the wall of the churchyard of St. Lawrence, facing the street, and since fastened to the wall of the nave. It is similar to the figures of Mercury at Aldborough and on the Wall of Hadrian, and probably represents that god.—*Rev. George Wade, Vicar of St. Lawrence, York*, 1881.

No. 19. A sculptured tablet, 2ft. 3in. high by 22in. wide, in the Entrance Hall of the Museum, representing the sacrifice and mysteries of Mithras ; found in 1747, in digging for a cellar in a house in Micklegate, opposite to St. Martin's

c 2

church. Mithras is a Greek form of the Persian word signi-
fying the sun, the chief object of worship among the Persians.
But long before Mithraic rites were adopted by the Romans,
the ancient religious principles and practices of the Persians
had been greatly changed by the theological doctrines of
Zoroaster, and the introduction of the psychological opinions,
and the ascetic usages of the Indians. In simple inscriptions,
Mithras is identified with the sun, and acknowledged as the
invincible god. But in the sculptured tablets he appears in a
different character, as the first of the celestial beings, called
Izeds, or good genii, the source of light, and the dispenser of
fertility.

In this tablet, Mithras is the principal figure. He is
represented as a young man, clothed with a tunic, a mantle,
and trowsers, having on his head a Phrygian bonnet. He is
kneeling firmly on a prostrate bull, which he holds with his
left hand by the nostrils, while with his right hand, he plunges
a short sword or dagger into its neck. A dog and some other
animals are generally introduced, either licking up the blood
that flows from the wound, or attacking the belly of the bull,
but they are wanting in this tablet. Above these principal
figures are three busts ; one on the left wearing a radiated
crown, the symbol of the sun; two on the right, much
mutilated, but one of them evidently adorned with a crescent,
the symbol of the moon. These luminaries being thus represented in this tablet, Mithras is not here the sun, nor the bull
the moon, of which it is sometimes the emblem ; but the bull
is to be considered as symbolical of the generative and
renovating principle, and Mithras as the powerful and beneficent
Ized, by whose agency (symbolized by his seizing the bull and
shedding its blood) that principle is diffused through all the
kingdoms of nature. On each side of the principal group is
an attendant bearing a torch, the torch of one being inverted,

having the flame downwards, the torch of the other (not seen in this tablet, in consequence of its mutilated condition) erect, with the flame upwards : the former denoting the descent of the souls of men from the lunar region to the earth ; the other their ascent, when regenerated and purified, to their celestial and eternal abode. This course of purification is briefly indicated by the group in the lower part of the tablet ; where we see first, the mystagogue or spiritual director, wearing a mantle, initiating the aspirant by pouring water on his head. The aspirant next appears, standing in a vessel supposed to be filled with snow or cinders, attended by his guide. This was one of several painful austerities to which the aspirant submitted ; but there being no room in the tablet for the representation of all of them, this is to be considered as representing the whole series. Having, as it must be supposed, passed through all the trials by means of which the soul was to be regenerated, the aspirant is seen in the last portion of the group, conducted by the mystagogue to the chariot, in which he is to ascend, by way of the moon, to a state of immortal felicity.

The sacrifice of Mithras is represented as being performed in a cave ; and such, either natural or artificial, was the scene in which the Mithraic rites were celebrated. It is probable that an artificial cave or crypt had been formed, for the worship of Mithras, where this tablet was discovered ; but no appearance of such a structure is recorded.*—*Deposited in the Museum by the Dean and Chapter of York*, 1844.

No. 20. A headless figure† in white marble, finely cut, representing, probably, the Muse of Tragedy, 8in. high,

* This is figured in Wellbeloved's Eburacum, p. 75.

† In the Catalogue of the Bateman Collection, p. 261, is "A mutilated figure of a female, covered with drapery, resting against a Cippus ; 18in. high ; of Roman work, well cut in sandstone. Found in excavating for the Railway Station, York, 1841."

holding a mask in her right hand. Found in 1845, near the entrance through the City Wall into the old Goods Station. (In case J upstairs.)—*The Cook Collection*, 1872.

No. 21. A fragment of a dedicatory tablet, 3ft. broad by 15in. high. The building to which it was affixed appears to have been dedicated to the deities of a reigning emperor, and a goddess, whose name or title is lost. The inscription is late in date; and of the name of the person by whom it was dedicated, the termination *sius* only remains. Perhaps we have in it the cognomen Numisius?

NVMINIB AVG ET DEAE IOV. . .
SIVS AEDEM PRO PARTE D. . .

This fragment was found in 1843 with No. 9, under the Yorkshire Bank in High Ousegate.—*The Hargrove Collection*, 1847.

No. 22. A dedicatory tablet, 3ft. 1in. wide, by 2ft. 1in. high, found in digging a cellar in Tanner-Row, in 1770, bearing the following inscription:

DEO ·SANCTO
SERAPI
TEMPLVM. A SO
LO FECIT
CL. HIERONY
MIANVS. LEG.
LEG. VI. VIC

On each side of the inscription are two *caducei*, a moon-shaped shield and a star.* The temple of Serapis is supposed to have stood near the old North Eastern Railway Hotel. A portion of a pavement from that site is in the Upper Room of the Hospitium. The name Hieronymianus occurs on an inscription found some years ago at Northallerton.—*The Corporation of York*, 1833.

* Figured in Wellbeloved's Eburacum, p. 75, where there is an interesting account of the fortunes of this tablet.

No. 23. A small, badly-wrought, altar, 11in. by 6in., found at the Station of Magna (Caervoran) on the Roman Wall in Northumberland.* It is inscribed :

DEO VETE
RI. NEO
ALA MIL
V. S. L. M.

Several altars dedicated to this divinity have been found at Caervoran, and many others on the line of the Roman Wall. They are now considered to refer to the ancient god or gods, as if a struggle had begun between the worship of the old deities and the new.

Ala mil. are supposed by Mr. Wellbeloved to denote *ala milliaria,* or *millenaria,* a squadron of double the usual number, which was 500. This reading is very questionable. Dr. Bruce considers that in the letters we have the names of the dedicator of the altar. An animal is rudely cut on the side, which Mr. Wellbeloved considers to be a horse, Dr. Bruce, probably, the sacrificial ox.—*Mr. Edwin Smith of Acomb,* 1846.

No. 24. A small altar, 11in. high by 4½in., found in the garden of St. Mary's Convent, Oct., 1880. It is thus inscribed :

DEO VE
TERI
PRIMVL
VS VOL.
M.

This is dedicated to the same deity as No. 23, by a person of the name of Primulus Volusianus, or Volusius. The last letter may, perhaps, be an abbreviation for *Merito,* but this is very doubtful, indeed it may perhaps be an addition of a later date. This altar is placed in the Hall of the Museum.— *The Superioress of St. Mary's Convent, York, Feb.* 1881.

* Engraved in Dr. Bruce's Lapidarium, p. 162; also in the Journal Arch. Assn., iii. 124, from a drawing sent by Mr. Wellbeloved.

No. 25. A large altar, 2ft. 3½in. high by 1ft. 4in. wide, found in Jan. 1874, under the archway leading from the Old to the New Station. It has no inscription but bears a garland on one side and a sacrificial axe on the other.—*The Directors, N. E. Railway Company*, 1874.

No. 26. A plain but finely cut altar of limestone, found in 1840, on the line of Railway near Holgate Bridge. It is 20in. high by about 12in. wide.—*The Hargrove Collection*, 1847.

No. 27. An altar, 19in. high by 12½in. wide, found at Wyke near Harewood. It has an ornament like a wheel on one side, and a sacrificial knife on the other.—*Edward Hailstone, F.S.A.*, 1864.

No. 28. A small altar, 16in. by 9½in., found under the donor's house in Bootham.—*J. H. Gibson, M.D.*, 1875.

No. 29. A part of a small but highly-ornamented altar, 10in. by 11in. in height, found in 1872, near the City Wall on the road towards the new Coal Depot. On one side is a *simpulum*, on the other what seems to have been a vase. The inscription has perished through the decay of the stone.—*The Directors, N. E. Railway*, 1872.

No. 30. A plain altar, 18in. high by 11in. in width, found at Temple Hill, near Bishopthorpe.—*Mr. Calvert, Bishopthorpe*, 1865.

No. 31. A small altar,* 14½in. high by 8in. in breadth, found in 1851 by a person digging for sand on the South side of Dunnington Common, near York. On one side are cut an axe and a knife. *W. Procter, M.D.*, 1851.

No. 32. The greater part of a large inscribed tablet of limestone, 3ft. 9in. by 3ft. 4in., discovered in 1854 by some workmen whilst digging a drain in King's Square (the old Curia Regis) at a depth of about 28ft. The inscription is

* Engraved in Bowman's Reliquiæ Eboracenses, p. 86.

arranged in six lines : the letters, beautifully cut, vary in
height, from 6in. to 3¼in.   In its perfect state the inscription
was probably as follows, the missing letters being supplied in
italics :

IMP CAESAR *DIVI*
*N*ERVAE. FIL. *NERVA TRA*
*IA*NVS. AVG. GER*M. DAC.*
*P*ONTIFEX MAXIMV*S TRIBVN.*
*P*OTESTATIS XII. I*MP. VI. COS V. P.P,*
PER. LEG. VIIII. HIS*P.*

Which may be thus rendered :

" The Emperor Cæsar Nerva Trajan, son of the deified
Nerva, Augustus, Germanicus, Dacicus, Chief Pontiff, invested
the twelfth time with the Tribunitian Powers, Consul the fifth
time, Father of his country, caused this to be performed by
the Ninth Legion (called) the Spanish."

What the work was that the Ninth Legion performed by
order of the Emperor cannot be ascertained ; but from the
character of the tablet it may be inferred that it was of
magnitude and importance.   As it was found in the old Curia
Regis, it is quite possible that it recorded the erection of the
Imperial Palace.

This is one of the most ancient of Roman inscriptions in
Britain ; the circumstances in the history of Trajan mentioned
on the tablet synchronizing with the years 108—109 of the
Christian era.   At that time the Ninth Legion came to York
and immediately set to work at the Emperor's bidding.   This
tablet assures to Éburacum an earlier foundation than used to
be ascribed to it.   It is evident that in A.D. 108—109 it was a
walled city and a place of importance in the empire, probably
even then the capital of Britain.   It may be assumed, therefore,
that it owed its origin, some forty years before the date of this
tablet, to the genius of Agricola.*—*The Corporation of York,*
1854.

* *cf.* Dr. Hübner's valuable note in his Inscrr. Brit. p. 64; Proc. of Y. P. S., i.
282, etc.; where this inscription is figured.

No. 33. A fragment of an inscription on limestone, 10in. by 6in., in beautiful characters, found in 1879, at the North end of the building for the Fine Art Exhibition :

TRAI

VG. P

These few letters seem to be a part of the usual formula observable in the inscriptions of Hadrian, which probably, when complete, ran as follows in an extended form : *Imperatori Cæsari divi Traiani Parthici filio, divi Nervæ nepoti, Traiano, Hadriano Augusto, pontifici maximo, tribunitia potestate . . consule . . , patri patriæ*—then came, probably, the title of the dedicator, a person, or a military body. It is much to be desired that some other portions of this inscription may be discovered. *The Committee of the Fine Art Exhibition,* 1879.

No. 34. A stone, 9in. long by 4in. high, with the letter A upon it, in relief; from the Roman Wall near the Multangular Tower on the N.W.

When this Tower was cleared out in 1831, nine other inscriptions were found, but they were, for the most part, rude scratchings, indicating the presence of the soldiers of the Sixth Legion. In one instance, a centurion of the name of Antonius was mentioned. These inscriptions are recorded in Mr. Wellbeloved's Eboracum, from which work Dr. Hübner has taken them. They have long since disappeared through exposure to the weather. It is impossible to represent them in this Catalogue except by an engraving.

No. 35. A large monumental stone, 6ft. 2in. high by 2ft. 2in. wide, on which is the figure of a Standard-bearer, in an arched recess. In his right hand he holds the Standard or Signum of the cohort, ending in an open hand, in his left an object about which there has been some doubt. It has been considered by Horsley and others that it represents the vessel used in measuring the corn, which was part of the Roman

45

soldiers' pay ;* but Dr. Hübner and Mr. Price have shown
satisfactorily that it is a collection of tablets or the wooden box
which contained them.† The following is the inscription :

L. DVCCIVS
L. VOLTRVFI
NVS. VIEN
SIGNIF. LEG. VIIII
AN. XXIIX
H. S. E.

which may be read : *Lucius Duccius, Lucii (filius), Voltinia
(Tribu), Rufinus, Viennensis, signifer legionis nonæ, annorum
viginti octo, hic situs est: i.e. Lucius Duccius Rufinus, son of
Lucius, of the Voltinian tribe, of Vienna, (in Gaul,) standard-
bearer of the Ninth Legion, aged twenty-eight, is buried here.*

This stone was found about the year 1686, probably where
it had been originally placed, in Trinity Gardens, Micklegate,
and was for a long time inserted in the church yard wall :‡
afterwards it was removed to Ribston Hall, the residence of the
Goodrickes, where it continued in the garden wall, exposed to the
weather until 1847. Dr. Hübner thinks that this is a monument
of the first century.—*Mr. Joseph Dent, of Ribston Hall, 1847.*

** A portion of a monumental tablet, 1ft. 10in. wide by about
1ft., found without Micklegate Bar, circa 1840, and now lost.
It represented the middle portion of the figure of a man holding
an object similar to that in the hand of the Standard-bearer.
Mr. John Browne, very fortunately, took a sketch of the
fragment of which there is a lithograph in Mr. Wellbeloved's
Eburacum, p. 115.

* See Mr. Price's Excavations in Camomile Street, Bishopsgate, pp. 45—7.
† A similar monument, on which the Standard-bearer is represented with the
same object in his left hand, was found in Camomile Street, London, and has
been described and illustrated by Mr. Price in the Transactions of the London
and Middlesex Archæological Society. The York monument has been engraved as
an illustration, and a copy of it is hung in the Upper Room of the Hospitium.
‡ cf. MS. Drake, xvi. 1. 2. in the York Minster Library. See also Thoresby's
Ducatus Leodiensis, 2nd ed., App. iij. Dr. Hübner (Inscrr. Brit. 64) shows that
this monument is known throughout Europe.

No. 36. A portion of a monumental tablet, 2ft. 8in. high by 2ft. 5in. wide, found on the Mount, in 1852, and thus inscribed. Some letters are added in italics.

```
          .....O·C·FIL
          NOVARIA         .
        MIL-LEG IX HISP·HERE
        DES ET LIB · PATRONO
       BENE MERENTI FECERVNT.
```

In the second line Dr. Hübner suggests the reading *Claud. Novaria*, as Novara was assigned to the Claudian Tribe. On the other hand the missing word may be a name, as in a similar inscription at Rome : " *C. Livius, C. F.; Justus, Novaria, Mil. Cho. IIII*, etc. Novare or Novara is a town near Milan.—*The Driffield Collection*, 1860.

No. 37. The upper part of a large sepulchral monument, representing a full-length figure in a recess, in high relief and finely carved, 4ft. high by 2ft. 7in. On the rim above the head of the figure, is the head of an ox. Dr. Hübner considers that it is the representation of a centurion, and that he holds in his right hand some vine twigs, and a book or roll in his left. It is much to be regretted that the inscription is missing which would give an account of the names and office of the deceased. This stone was found on the Mount in 1852.—*The Driffield Collection*, 1860.

No. 38. A funereal stone, of which two parts only out of four are preserved, 30in. long by 26in. wide. They were probably a part of the Driffield collection and were found, therefore, on the Mount. The inscription runs thus :

```
            M.
            LIVS
          CRESCES
          A. VET
      LEG. (VI.) VIC.
        CA . . . . . .
      PRI . . . . . .
      ETM . . . . . .
```

It is evident that the monument is to . . Manlius Cresce(n)s, a veteran of the Sixth Legion, and that it was set up by his heirs, to one of whom Dr. Hübner tentatively gives the names of Cæcilius Primitivus. In the missing part of the third and fourth lines the name of the father of the deceased may have been given with his tribe.—*The Driffield Collection*, 1860.

No. 39. A large tablet, 5ft. 8in. high and 3ft. broad, found in use as a cover to the sarcophagus of Ælia Severa (No. 47). The upper part of the slab shows the figures of a father and mother and two children. The inscription is faint, and, as far as it can be read, is as follows:

> D.M. FLAVIÆ AVGVSTINÆ
> VIXIT. AN. XXXVIIII. M. VII. D. XI. FILIVS
> . —VS .AVGSTINVS. VIXIT. AN. I. D III
> . . . . . VIXIT. AN. I. M VIIII. D V.C. ÆRESIVS
> . . . . MIL. LEG. VI. VIC. CONIVGI. CAR
> FILIIS. ET. SIBI. F. C.

It appears that C. Æresius* . . . . , a soldier of the Sixth Legion victorious, raised this memorial to his wife, Flavia Augustina, who lived thirty-nine years, seven months, and eleven days; to his son . . . Augustinus, who lived one year and three days; and to a daughter, who lived one year, nine months, and five days; providing at the same time a memorial for himself. It is probable that the missing name of the son was Flavius. The stone was found on the Mount.—*Mr. John Jones*, 1859.

No. 40. A finely-wrought coffin, 4ft. by 2ft., found in the excavation for the N.E. Railway, near Holgate Bridge. It bears the following beautifully simple inscription:

> D.M. SIMPLICIAE FLORENTINE
> ANIME INNOCENTISSIME
> QVE VIXIT MENSES DECEM
> FELICIVS. SIMPLEX. PATER. FECIT
> LEG. VI. V.

---

* *cf.* Dr. Mc Caul's Britanno-Roman Inscriptions, pp. 217—19.

"*To the Gods, the Manes. To Simplicia Florentina, a most innocent being, who lived ten months, Felicius Simplex her father, of the Sixth Legion Victorious, dedicated this.*" No mother's name appears; a circumstance which suggests the probability of the birth of this darling child having been marked by a lamentable event that gives still greater interest to this tribute of paternal affection. It is remarkable also that the words "*anime innocentissime*" are found on the Christian tombs in the Catacombs, a fact which opens out a most interesting field of thought.—*The Directors of the N.E. Railway*, 1837.

No. 41. A large coffin of coarse grit, 7½ft. long by 2ft. 11in., found whilst excavating the Castle Yard, in 1835, and thus inscribed in a panel:

D.   M.
AVR. SVPERO. CENT
LEG. VI. QVIVIXITANIS
XXXVIII. MIIII. DXIII. AVRE
LIA. CENSORINA. CONIVNX
MEMORIAM. POSSVIT.

"*To the Gods, the Manes.* To Aurelius Superus, a Centurion of the Sixth Legion, who lived thirty-eight years, four months, and thirteen days, Aurelia Censorina, his wife, set up this memorial.*"

Another coffin, found by the side of this, is in the Multangular Tower. Two skulls found in them are in the possession of the Society.—*The Magistrates of the North Riding of Yorkshire*, 1839.

No. 42. A fragment of a sepulchral tablet, 12in. high by 16in., found on the Mount and thus inscribed:

. . . . . . SECVN
. . . . . L. VOCO

* The word *Manes* denotes the souls of the departed; "but as it is a natural tendency to consider the souls of departed friends as blessed spirits, they were called by the Romans Dii Manes, and were worshipped with divine honors."
The skull found in this coffin is preserved in the Museum.

49

Mr. Thompson Watkin in a paper on the Roman forces in Britain says, that the Ala Augusta Vocontiorum,* according to an inscription found in Holland, was a cavalry force in the army in Britain. In the second line of this inscription, Mr. Watkin thinks that it is mentioned, and regards the L. as the second letter of AL. or ALAE. This is probable enough. The Title of Augusta is missing, but this is not always inserted. The name of deceased seems to have been Secundus or Secundinus, an eques in the Vocontian Ala. Above the inscription are two beasts seated, with a cub—probably a family of lions or leopards.—*The Driffield Collection*, 1860.

No. 43. The sarcophagus of a Decurion of the Colony of Eboracum, 7ft. long by 3ft. 6in. high, discovered in 1872, near the Scarborough railway bridge, on a site where other inscribed stones have been found, and more may be looked for. The coffin, which by an unfortunate accident, was greatly injured in the course of removal, bears an inscription in very faint and late characters :

D.   M.
FLAVI BELLATORIS DEC. COL. EBORACENS
VIXIT ANNIS XXVIIII. MENS . . .
. . . .

A third line is wholly illegible. This inscription is of great importance, as it ascertains the fact that Eburacum was a *municipium*, which was not previously known. The decurions constituted a civic council or senate, to which the title of *splendidissimus ordo* was applied.† A gold ring set with a ruby was found upon the finger of the decurion, who was a person of small stature ‡—*The Directors of the N.E. Railway Company*, 1872.

* This Ala is mentioned in an inscription found in Scotland. *cf.* Hübner, No. 1080. It is there styled Ala Augusta Vocontiorum. .

† See a paper by Mr. Kenrick in *Proceedings of the Y.P.S.*, 8vo, 1855, pp. 52—65; Grüter. DCIX. 3 ; Smith's Coll. Ant., V. p. 19.

‡ The skull found in the coffin is in the possession of the Society.

** A stone coffin, found in February, 1579-80, about a quarter of a mile to the West of the Walls of York. In the following century it was carried to Hull and was used as a horse-trough at an inn called the Coach and Horses, in Beverleygate. All traces of the coffin have disappeared. It seems to have borne the following inscription :

M. VEREC. DIOGENES. IIIIIIVIR COL.
EBOR. IBIDEMQ. MORT. CIVES BITVRIX
CVBVS. HAEC SIBI. VIVVS FECIT.

In the inscription the word *ibidem* seems to have appeared in a contracted form. Professor Hübner[*] suggests the reading *itemq(ue) m(unicipii) Orit* (   ) as if Diogenes had been the Sevir of another municipality in addition to York. Mr. Kenrick[†] follows Horsley in preferring the reading *ibidemque mortuus*, as if the coffin had been prepared by Diogenes during his life, and the inscription cut by his heir after his decease. I do not see, however, why the inscription should not have been cut during the life of Diogenes, notwithstanding the fact that the stone records the place of his death ; especially as the presumption is that he prepared a coffin for his wife while she was alive. An heir would have put upon each coffin the age of the person interred in it. The health of M. Diogenes, when he prepared the stone, may have been such that he would know of a certainty that he never could leave Eburacum alive. The Bituriges Cubi, of which people M. Verec. Diogenes was a citizen, lived in Celtic Gaul. Their chief town, Avaricum, or Bourges, was stormed by Cæsar, who regarded it as one of the fairest cities in the country. Diogenes was a Sevir, or Sexvir, of York. The Seviri formed a college or legal corporation, the duties of which are still very imperfectly known. They seem to have been taken from the more wealthy tradesmen, and to have had much to do with public works of various kinds. In rank they were inferior to the Decurions.

This was the first inscription from which it became known that Eburacum was a *Colonia*. This fact and the correctness in the main of the reading of this inscription, have been placed beyond dispute by recent discoveries. There is a drawing of this monument among the Stukeley Letters, which will soon be published by the Surtees' Society.

No. 44. A large stone coffin, 7ft. long by 2ft. 4in. in depth, with an inscription well and deeply cut; discovered in March, 1877, about a quarter-of-a-mile from the City Walls, in the course of the excavation for the North Eastern Railway. It was within a few yards of the coffin of Bellator the Decurion. The inscription is as follows :

IVL. FORTVNATE . DOMO
SARDINIA . VEREC . DIO
GENI FIDA CONIVNCTA
MARITO.

There can be no doubt that we have here the tomb of the wife of the Sevir of York, who has just been mentioned. Julia Fortunata, was, it appears, a native of Sardinia, and it is extremely probable, from the inscription itself, that this memorial was prepared for her by her husband during her life. The tomb contained the perfect skeleton of a somewhat tall person. This is the finest, and in some respects the most interesting sepulchral memorial that the Museum possesses.*
The Directors of the North Eastern Railway, 1877.

No. 45. The greater part of a striking monument, 3ft. high by 2ft. 3in. wide, to commemorate a child. The father and mother are represented sitting in an alcove. A young girl stands at one end of the couch, and a tripod table, with a cake or loaf of bread upon it, is in front. The right arm of the

* The skull found in this coffin is preserved in the Museum.

husband is passed around the neck of the wife. She holds a
wine cup in her hand, and a small hooped wine-cask lies on
the floor. The husband holds something in his hand resembling a roll. Below is this inscription :

AELIÆ ÆLIANÆ
VIX. ANN.

The fracture of the stone has destroyed the rest of the
inscription. The monument has been supposed to represent
a simple meal, as typical of domestic affection. It is remarkable that the bronze shield of a soldier called Ælius Ælianus
was found some time ago in a moss near Thorsbjerg in
Schleswig. It is described in Engelhardt's Denmark in
the Early Iron Age, p. 49, plate 8. This stone was found in
the old Cricket field whilst excavating for the new Railway
Station.—*The Directors of the N.E. Railway*, 1872.

No. 46. A fragment of a monumental stone, 2ft. wide by
1ft. 8in., on which a female is represented as reclining on a
couch, and holding a small cup in her left hand. This is
evidently a portion of a monument similar to that of Ælia
Æliana.

No. 47. A large sarcophagus found on the Mount, 7ft. 4in.
long by 2ft. 4in. wide, and inscribed :

D. ÆL. SEVERE. HONESTE. FEMINE M
CONIVGI. CA C. RVFI. QVOND
V.AN.XXVII.M.VIIII·D·IIII. CÆC
MVSICVS. LIB. EIVS. D.

It is dedicated to the Manes of Ælia Severa, who died, aged
twenty-seven years, eight months, and four days, and had
once been the wife of Cæcilius Rufus. Cæcilius Musicus, her
freedman (her husband being dead) erected this monument to
her memory. It was common for slaves on their emancipation
to take the prænomen of their masters. When found the
letters were still filled with *minium* or red paint, and the
sarcophagus was covered by No. 39. The skeleton in it,

which was laid in gypsum, appeared to be that of a male, so that it is probable that coffin as well as cover had been appropriated to some later interment.—*Mr. John Jones*, 1859.

No. 48. The larger portion of a small monumental stone, 8in. by 13in. wide, found in the road in front of the New Railway Station. It bears the following inscription, the letters within brackets being supplied :

MEMORIAE.

. . . . . DASSAEI. IVLI.

[ET. FE] LICIS. FILI. SVI.

[D] VLCISSI [MI]

.   .   .   .   .   .

.   .   .   .   .   .

The names on this monument are common in epigraphy.—*The Directors of the N.E. Railway*, 1874.

No. 49. A sepulchral monument, 4ft. high by 2ft. wide, discovered in 1861, on the Mount, on the left hand side of the road to Tadcaster. It was erected by Q. Corellius Fortis to the memory of his daughter Corellia Optata, who died at the age of thirteen. When perfect, it had at the top a sculptured figure, of which only the feet remain. The inscription, extended, reads as follows :

(D.)   M.

CORELLIA. OPTATA. AN. XIII.

SECRETI. MANES. QVI. REGNA ACHERVSIA. DITIS.

INCOLITIS. QVOS. PARVA. PETVNT POST LVMINA. VITE.

EXIGVVS. CINIS ET. SIMVLACRVM. CORPO[R]IS. VMBRA.

INSONTIS GNATE. GENITOR. SPE. CAPTVS. INIQVA

SVPREMVM. HVNC. NATE MISERANDVS. DEFLEO FINEM

Q. CORE. FORTIS. PAT. F.C.

A large glass vessel, containing the ashes of the young girl, and some pottery were found with this stone. Is the father the person whose name occurs on so many lamps ? They certainly appear to be of local manufacture.—*Mr. John Rush*, 1863.

D

No. 50. The upper part of a monument, 1ft. 9in. wide by
1ft. 10in. high, found when deepening a cellar at St. Mary's
Convent. The top is ornamented with a small bust of the
deceased, with a basket filled with fruit on one side, and a
chaplet of laurel on the other :

D. M.

DECIMINAE. DE

CIMI   FILIAE.

The lower part of the stone probably contained the age of
Decimina, with an expression of parental affection and regret.—
The Superioress of St. Mary's Convent, York, 1860.

No. 51. Two small portions of a monument, 21in. broad
by 17in. high, which fit together, but do little more than reveal
one of the probable names of the deceased person, Gabinia :

M.

. . . . ABINIA

Above the inscription, in a sunk panel, was some sculpture,
of which a fish is the sole remnant. Found on the Mount.—
The Driffield Collection, 1860.

No. 52. A cippus, or monumental pillar, 4ft. 6in. in height
by 16in. in width, of a circular form, the upper part in front
having been cut away to give a smooth face for an inscription,
which was, unhappily, almost obliterated by the carelessness of
the finders. The only words that are legible are :

HYLLO

ALVMNO

CARISSIMO

....

....

It is remarkable that this monument corresponds in a very
singular manner, both in inscription and form, with another
discovered at Plumpton, in Cumberland, which is figured in
Dr. Bruce's Lapidarium Septentrionale, p. 409.* It is

* Dr. Hübner gives the inscription *D. M. Ylæ alumni Karissimi. Vixit annis
XIII. Claudius Severus* . . . . (pp. 79 and 113.)

probable that the two commemorate two foster-children, Hyllus and Hylas, of some officer or soldier quartered at York, one of whom died at head-quarters, and the other at a distant camp. The York monument was found in one of the docks in the New Railway Station.—*The Directors N.E. Railway*, 1875.

** On a stone, now lost, formerly in a wall on the Mount, was the following fragmentary inscription :

D. M.
MINNE.

The name occurs in inscriptions. This stone is mentioned by Dean Gale and others, and there is a drawing of it among Dr. Stukeley's correspondence.

No. 53. The remains of a coffin, 6ft. 10in. long, by 2ft. 3in., found about the beginning of the present century, in the garden of Mr. Robert Driffield, on the Mount, bearing the following inscription :

MEM. · AL. THEODORI
ANI. NOMENT. VIXIT. ANN
XXXV. .M. VI. EMI. THEO
DORA. MATER. E. C.

The interpretation of Dr. Hübner is the best that has been given : *Memoriæ Valeriani Theodoriani Nomentani. Vixit annos XXXV menses VI. Emi Theodora mater ejus causa.* Theodorianus was a native of Nomentum, in Italy, and the coffin which held his remains, was purchased* by his mother, Theodora. The skull discovered in this coffin, which is of noble proportions, is in the possession of Mr. W. Driffield, of Huntington.—*The Driffield Collection*, 1860.

No. 54. A fragment (about one third) of a sepulchral inscription, 25in. high by 17in., much decayed, removed in 1867 from the south wall of the Parish Church of All Saints, North Street, where it was observed in 1682. It appears to have been a memorial of affection by a Roman of the name of

* *cf.* McCaul's Britanno-Roman Inscriptions, pp. 213—15.

Antonius to his wife. The following are all the letters that can be made out, the first is defective :

```
. . . M.
. . . AE. AN
. . . S. SEC.
. . . ENTE M
. . . I. ANTO
. . . CONIVG I
```

An Antonius, a prefect of the soldiers, was mentioned in a rude inscription in the Multangular Tower. On each side of the inscription there has been a winged figure.—*Rev. G. W. Guest, Rector of All Saints, North Street,* 1867.

No. 55. A part of a small monument, 10in. high by 16in. broad, found in a heap of stones at Clementhorpe by Mr. R. H. Skaife, where it had been some time in use as a building-stone. The first line of the inscription has been squared off by some mediæval mason :

```
FIL. V. AN. XIII.
VITELLIA PRO
CVLA MATER
P. P. F.
```

The three letters at the end were read by Mr. Kenrick, P.P.F., *i.e., propria pecunia,* or *pro pietate, fecit.* Dr. Hübner thinks they may have been F.P.F., *filia piissimæ, fecit.* In a corner of the stone are two mediæval letters, A(ve) M(aria), designed, no doubt, to take away any evil influences which might result from the heathen inscription.—*Mr. John Braddock,* 1865.

No. 56. A fragment of a monumental inscription found on the Mount, 21in. broad by 15in. :

```
M.
. . . VIVS FE
. . . . VS
```

The *M.* is imperfect. The person may have been called Julius or Salvius Felix, or some such names.—*The Driffield Collection,* 1860.

No. 57. Two fragments of what must have been an important inscription. They fit together and are 20in. broad by 11in. high, and are cut on smooth limestone in beautiful letters, not later in date than the end of the second century. They were found in 1843, at the corner of High Ousegate and Nessgate, under the present Yorkshire Bank :

```
. . . . . . . . . . O . . . . .
. . . . . . . . I. P.P. SVB. . .
. . . . RI. ET. M. COSS. . . . .
```

The two last lines would have given some valuable information, including, most probably, the names of a Roman legate. The last words may have been after this fashion, *Sub cura Julii Severi et Marci Cossutii . . .*—*The Hargrove Collection*, 1847.

No. 58. A fragment of a monument found in the new road from the Mount to Clementhorpe in 1877. It is well cut in limestone, 9in. square, and is of the time of Trajan or Hadrian. The portion preserved gives the end of the last two lines :

CVR
D.S.P.

In an extended form, perhaps, the letters may be read *(fieri) curavit de sua pecunia.* The D however may be an O.—*The Corporation of York*, 1877.

No. 59. The upper part of a sepulchral monument, 2ft. 6in. wide by 3ft. 1in high, found in 1839 under the City Wall in excavating for the Railway. It represents, probably, a father and a son. The man holds a staff in his right hand, and a book (?) in his left. The child has hold of his father's dress with one hand and has a basket in the other.* In one corner the letter M, for *Manibus*, remains, and nothing more. *The Directors of the N.E. Railway*, 1839.

* In the base of the tower of the church of St. Martin in Micklegate, on the West side, is a portion of a sepulchral memorial, representing the lower part of three figures, two adults and a child. Other Roman sculptured stones are near it.

No. 60.   A very peculiar stone, 2ft. high, representing a head with long hair.   Below, on a double face, angle-wise, are the letters :

DM   CE.

The stone perhaps stood at one of the corners of a large square tomb, the principal inscription being in the centre below.   It is to be presumed that D.M. may be expanded into *Diis Manibus*.   Do C.E. refer to the names of the defunct, or can they represent *Cives Eburacenses*, or, *Colonia Eburacensis?*   The head is probably that of one of the Deities or Genii of the lower world.   This curious stone was found at the bottom of an old wall in Castlegate in 1879.— *Purchased*, 1879.

No. 61.   A number of fragments of a large inscription found in the garden in front of the New Station Hotel, in 1878.   The inscription seems to have been on the sides of a square block, above which was a figure, of which all that remains is a hand resting on a cushion.   On one fragment is the word AVG.   On another, at the end of the uppermost line, are the letters ISIV., which may be compared with No. 21.   We perhaps have in these letters the cognomen, Numisius.   *The Directors of the N.E. Railway*, 1878.

No. 62.   A large coarse boulder stone, 3½ft. by 2ft. broad, found circa 1810, in the foundation of a wall at Hazlehead near Whitby.   On the side of it is an inscription in rough, tall letters, the upper part of which has shaled off, rendering the letters illegible.   There is an engraving of the stone in Young's History of Whitby, p. 703, who connects it with the Sixth Legion.—*Mr. Alfred Foster of Egton*, 1876.

No. 63.   A sculptured stone, representing a smith, holding in his right hand a hammer, and in his left a pair of tongs, with which he lays a piece of iron on an anvil.   It was found at Dringhouses, near the Roman road to Calcaria (Tadcaster), and probably was the memorial of an armourer of one of the legions quartered at York.—*Dr. Eason Wilkinson*, 1860.

No. 64. Three small stone cists or coffins for children, found whilst excavating for the New Railway Station. They average about 3ft. in length. An impression in gypsum of the body of one of the children is preserved in the upper room.— *The Directors of the N.E. Railway*, 1873, *etc*.

No. 65. A very large and ponderous stone coffin, nearly 8ft. long by 3ft. in height, found in 1877, in one of the docks in the New Railway Station. A glass lid has been placed on the coffin to show the skeleton which is laid in gypsum. Some portions of the linen in which the corpse was wrapped were found adhering to the gypsum, and are exhibited in the upper room of the Hospitium. The coffin has been wrought by a left-handed mason, a fact which was discovered by a brother in the same craft labouring under a similar infirmity, when he was fastening the wooden frame to the stone.—*The Directors of the N.E. Railway*, 1877.

No. 66. A stone coffin, 7ft. 2in. long, found in 1875 under the Booking Office of the New Railway Station. It contains a coffin of lead, 6ft. long, with a corded pattern impressed upon it. Inside this, imbedded in gypsum, were the remains of a lady, whose hair containing two jet pins was most fortunately preserved.* This is exhibited in the upper room.—*The Directors of the N.E. Railway*, 1875.

No. 67. A large coffin of lead, 6ft. 7in. long, with the skeleton in it, discovered during the excavations for the Old Railway Station, circa 1840. The end of the coffin is rolled over the skull.—*The Directors of the N.E. Railway*.

* For an account of this remarkable discovery, *cf.* the Transactions of the Y.P.S. for 1875. The ornamented lid of the lead coffin is figured in Mr. C. R. Smith's Collectanea, vii., pt. iii., p. 178. *cf.* Journal Arch. Assn. ii., 297, and xiv. 337. Smith's Collectanea, iii. 49—62. A valuable paper by Dr. Procter on the Metallurgy of Lead is in the Transactions of the Society.

No. 68.   A large lead coffin, 6ft. 4in. long, enclosed originally in a shell of wood, found on the site of the New Railway Station.   Portions of the iron tire which bound the wood and lead together are preserved in the Museum.   *The Directors of the North Eastern Railway*, 1873.

No. 69.   The remains of a coffin, 6ft. 2in. long, and 21in. wide, originally of wood lined with thin sheets of lead, bound together with strong clasps and bars of iron.   The wooden coffin has been restored, but with a glass lid to show the skeleton and the leaden lining, and over all have been placed the iron bands in the position in which they were found.   The coffin was found in 1875 under the New Railway Station, and is figured in Mr. C. R. Smith's Collectanea, vii. pt. iii. p. 179.   *The Directors of the North Eastern Railway*, 1875.

No. 70.   A Roman tomb, made of bricks and covered with tiles, found under the New Railway Station in 1875.   The dimensions are 7ft. 4in. in length, 3ft. 1in. in breadth, and 1ft. 6in. in height.   In the interior were some remains of a coffin of wood, containing the bones of an aged person.   The tomb is very carefully set up with the old materials, the mortar alone being new, but it is made of the same material as the old, and is of the same thickness.   The covering tiles bear the mark of their maker, and have been impressed by the feet of a dog and its puppies which had run over the tiles when they were wet.*   *The Directors of the North Eastern Railway*, 1875.

---

* Under the houses on the Mount now occupied by Messrs. Flower and Milner, is a large domed vault of brick, 8ft. long, 5ft. broad, aud 6ft. high, containing a beautifully wrought coffin of stone. This was discovered in 1807, and has often been visited by the curious. A great portion of the vault must have been originally above the surface of the ground. *cf.* Archæologia, xvi, 340, and Wellbeloved's Eburacum, p. 107.

A brick tomb, somewhat similar to that now preserved in the Museum, was found in 1840, during the excavations for the Railway. It was 8ft. 6in. long and 4ft. 6in. wide, with a domed roof. It contained the skeleton of a female laid in

No. 71. The greater part of a tomb, 5ft. long, composed of twelve tiles, found in 1840, when excavating for the Railway, outside the city walls. The tiles are stamped LEG. IX. HISP.,* so that it is probable that the tomb covered a soldier of the Ninth, or Spanish Legion.—*The Hargrove Collection*, 1847.

No. 72. A tomb, composed of 18 tiles, 7ft. 6in. long, discovered in 1833, near Dringhouses, on the road to Tadcaster, formed of roof-tiles (*tegulæ*) and ridge-tiles (*imbrices*), which bear the impress of the Sixth Legion,†

LEG. VI. VI.

erected, it is probable, over the ashes of a soldier of that legion. Nothing was found in it but a layer of the remains of a funeral pile, consisting of charcoal and bones, about six inches in thickness, with several iron nails.—*Mr. Eshelby*, 1833.

No. 73. A portion of another tomb made of ten tiles, 5ft. 8in. long, found during the Railway Excavations in 1874. It is remarkable for having something like a cupola or turret at the head. Two plain urns were found at one end.—*The Directors of the North Eastern Railway*, 1874.

gypsum, with her hair preserved. The tomb was transferred to the garden of Mr. Hargrove's house in Blossom Street, and was set up as it was found, but all traces of it have disappeared.

* In the Archæologia, vol. ii., there is an account by Dr. White, of York, of the discovery of the tomb of some one connected with the same legion which contained several urns. In engraving of the tomb is appended to the wall of the Upper room.

† Another tomb, bearing the stamp, *LEG. VI. VIT. P. F*, and composed of twenty-one tiles was found during the Railway excavations at York, in September, 1845, and is now with the Bateman Collection, in the Sheffield Museum (Catalogue, p. 128) " The tiles were placed, as is usual, with the upper ends inclining together so as to leave a drain-like space, within which the skeleton was deposited with the head resting upon a semi-circular tile, inscribed like the others. When found, it was full of water which had percolated from the surface, a depth of about three feet." *cf.* Journal Archæological Association, i. 191-2.

A similar tomb was discovered during the Excavations for the New Railway Station, in 1873. The tiles, all of which were broken, bore the stamp of the Sixth Legion. In the tomb were found eight or ten glass vessels, two of which are in the Museum.

D 2

No. 74. A laureated head, 18in. high, found in excavating for a drain in Stonegate. The first Roman sculpture that the Society acquired.—*Mr. James Atkinson*, 1828.

No. 75. The head of a large statue, and a portion of a second, from the Driffield Collection. A third, the largest of the three and very rude, was found near the New Railway Station Hotel, in 1874.

No. 76. A small head of a marble figure, discovered on Toft Green in 1875. A foot was found at the same time. (In Case L upstairs).—*Purchased*, 1878.

No. 77. A fragment of a sculptured slab, representing part of a man's leg, and a foot with a sandal.—*The Driffield Collection*, 1860,

No. 78. Several Phallic sculptures discovered during the late Railway Excavations, and at other times.

No. 79. Four Cones of the Pine. The pine was sacred to the Phrygian goddess Cybele. The cone represented on funeral monuments is supposed to allude to the use of resinous wood in burning the body. The cone marked *a* is from the Driffield Collection ; another marked *d*, was found in 1873, near the new Coal Depôt of the North Eastern Railway Company ; the largest of the five was found at Dringhouses, in 1878, and was acquired by purchase in 1881.

No. 80. A mutilated figure of a lion, 2ft. 8in. long, in act to spring, found in 1873, on the site of the New Railway Station. Such figures are considered to be Mithraic emblems.* *The Directors of the North Eastern Railway*, 1873.

No. 81. The head of a similar animal, 1ft. 4in. long.

No. 82. A large stone, 3ft. long by 1ft. wide, with the head of a dog in rude relief, found under the City Wall in 1839.—*The Directors of the North Eastern Railway*, 1839.

* *cf.* Mr. Price's Account of the Excavations in Camomile Street, pp. 60—65.

No. 83. Part of the tail of the figure of a sea-horse, or of some other imaginary marine monster, 2ft. 5in. long.—*From the Driffield Collection*, 1860.

No. 84. Figure of a Harpy, nearly entire, found on the Mount in 1852, and 2ft. 6in. high.—*From the Driffield Collection*, 1860.

No. 85. A Gorgon's head, 21in. square, vigorously but coarsely cut.

No. 86. Large fragments of sculptures, which probably formed part of the pediment of the Roman gateway, on the N.W. side of Eburacum ; or of some public building near it. They were found near Bootham Bar, where the foundations of the Roman gateway were discovered. One is a rude representation of a quadriga or chariot drawn by four horses: another of a Triton blowing his concha or shell trumpet: a third, a portion of an ornamented frieze : and a fourth, the figure of a sphinx or some imaginary animal. The base of a pier, found at the same place, probably belonged to the gateway.*—*Mr. Tilney*, 1835.

No. 87. A portion of a frieze, 18in. by 12in., showing a Cupid. Found near Micklegate Bar, in 1860.—*The Cook Collection*, 1872.

No. 88. A fragment found with many other Roman remains below one of the piers at the south end of the old bridge over the Ouse, in 1818. When perfect, it represented an eagle, with a wreath about the neck, within a wreath of laurel. It was obtained by Mr. B. Brooksbank, and placed in the hall of his mansion at Healaugh ; after his death it was presented to the Yorkshire Philosophical Society, by his son Mr. Stamp Brooksbank, in 1852.

* Some fragments of pillars were discovered here in 1877. There is some reason to believe that Bootham Bar is in its core a Roman gate.

No. 89. Fragment of a slab, 2ft. 10in. long, on which is the figure of an eagle.

No. 90. A portion of the architrave of a Roman doorway, 3ft. long, found below one of the piers of the old bridge, with many similar remains, which it was thought not desirable to remove.—*Mr. George Todd*, 1823.

No. 91. Fragments of pillars, one of which is 4ft. high, found in excavating for a drain in Micklegate, belonging, probably, to a Roman temple, or some other public building. Several other sculptured stones are preserved in the basement of the tower of the neighbouring church of St. Martin.—*The Corporation of York*, 1853.

No. 92. A fragment of a pillar, 2ft. 8in. high, ornamented with human heads, and basket work, over which a man is climbing. Found on the hill near the New Goods Station.— *The Directors of the North Eastern Railway*, 1876.

No. 93. A small capital of a pillar representing a man attacked by two lions. Found near the New Railway Station, in 1874.—*The Directors of the North Eastern Railway*, 1874.

No. 94. A small pillar-shaped stone, 1ft. 4in. high, found in 1843, under the Yorkshire Bank. It is a prop for a hypocaust.—*The Hargrove Collection*, 1847.

No. 95. The front part of the fire-place of a hypocaust as it was found amidst the foundations of the Roman baths, 3ft. 7in. high, and 4ft. 4in. wide at the top.—*The Directors of the North Eastern Railway*, 1839.

No. 96. Leaden pipes, found in the same place. *The Directors of the North Eastern Railway*, 1839.

No. 97. Two large pipes of lead, one of which is 9ft. long, found in Church Street, opposite Patrick Pool, in 1854.—*The Corporation of York*, 1854.

No. 98. Short pillars (pilæ), used in supporting the floors of the hot or vapour baths, with fragments of the plaster floor, discovered in excavating for the Old Railway Station.—*The Directors of the North Eastern Railway*, 1839.

No. 99. A piece of flooring from the Roman baths.—*The Directors of the North Eastern Railway*, 1839.

No. 100. A large piece of flooring, probably from the same source, found in December, 1873, under the City Wall, when the road was being made from the Old to the New Railway Station.—*The Directors of the North Eastern Railway*, 1873.

No. 101. A thick slab of concrete, 7ft. long, by 2ft. broad, with raised edges, and a groove in one corner. It is the bottom of a bath found in a Roman villa, at Dalton Parlours, near Collingham, which was excavated by the Society in 1854.* The pillars of the hypocaust are beside it in one of the lower rooms in the Museum. A tessellated pavement from the same place is shown in the upper room in the Hospitium.—*The Trustees of Lady Betty Hastings' Charity*, 1854.

No. 102. Part of a drain, 18in. square, found on the site of the Yorkshire Insurance Company, amongst the foundations of buildings supposed to have been attached to the gateway near the river, in the south-western wall of the Roman Station. This fragment is an interesting specimen of Roman sewerage, and at the same time illustrates the Roman method of constructing walls by alternate courses of brick and stone.—*The Yorkshire Insurance Company*, 1847.

II. ANGLO-SAXON.

Although the Angles, or Anglo-Saxons, had possession of York for more than four hundred years, comparatively few remains of their work have been discovered. They occupied, it is presumed, the buildings which the Romans and their immediate successors had used, and these, from various causes, have entirely disappeared. The principal edifice

* For an account of these Excavations, *cf.* a Selection of Papers of Y. P. S., 270.

erected during the Anglian period in the city was the
Minster, which was begun in the seventh century, and rebuilt
and enlarged by Archbishop Albert in the eighth. Some
remains of this may be seen in the crypts beneath the choir
of the present cathedral. In four only of the York churches
have any remains of Anglo-Saxon work been discovered,
although there is much, no doubt, beneath the soil, and built
up in the walls. We know from undoubted authority that
Eoferwic was one of the greatest cities in the country, and for
a long time the capital of the island. Within the last few
years a great cemetery of the Anglian period has been
discovered in the vicinity of the city, and many farther traces
of the Anglo-Saxon lords of Eoferwic will, no doubt, be found.
There is a still greater paucity of memorials of the Danish
occupation of York, which extended from the ninth century to
the eleventh. The Danish carving, however, cannot easily
be distinguished from the Anglo-Saxon, and among the
sculptured stones which we are about to describe, there are
some, no doubt, which belong to this period.

No. 1. Fragment of a pillar or cross, found in St. Leonard's
Place, near the site of the ancient Hospital of St. Peter,
having the following imperfect inscription :

ADM.

MORI

AM

S͞C͞O

RVM

. . . .

which may be read thus, AD MEMORIAM SANCTORUM.

No. 2. A curiously ornamented stone, found in the
excavations preparatory to the building of St. Leonard's
Place, near the site of the Hospital of St. Peter. It is the
fragment of a Saxon cross or pillar, having the figure of two
grotesque animals implicated in the slender spirally-disposed

branches of a tree or a shrub on one side, and common Saxon ornaments on the other sides.

No. 3.   A fragment exhibiting a kind of fretted work, and an animal supposed to represent a dragon.

No. 4.   A portion of a Saxon cross or pillar, found with several rude wooden coffins* and some other Saxon remains, in excavating for the New Market, or Parliament Street.   It is ornamented on three sides with the usual Saxon interlaced ribbon, with a bead-moulding.   The fourth side being plain, appears to indicate that it had been placed against a wall.

No. 5.   Two sepulchral stones, each bearing a rude cross, found in the excavations preparatory to the building of Parliament Street.

No. 6.   A coped and curiously ornamented lid of a Saxon coffin, found buried close to the south wall of what had been the nave of the church of St. Denis, Walmgate.   The sculpture is so much defaced, as to render it difficult to trace the whole of the original design.   On one side of the coping, near the centre, in the midst of much interlacing, the figure of a bird may be perceived, with the body of a reptile, or a part of the interlacing, in its beak ; and on the left of it, the head of some animal biting a sword.   On the other side, two animals, resembling bears, standing on their hind legs ; two groups of monsters ; a representation of the wolf and twins (the reverse of some of the late coins of the Romans, found also on Saxon coins†), and a human figure standing near them.   A spiral, cord-like moulding, runs along the ridge and the sides, forming the angle of the coping at each end.—*Purchased*, 1848.

No. 7.   An imperfect lid of a Saxon coffin, exhibiting in two compartments, extending along its whole length, the common

---

* Some of these coffins were discovered in 1878, under Messrs. Makins and Dean's shop.   The place marks the site of an ancient cemetery.

† Ruding, i., 101, 115.   Haigh, Coins of E. Anglia, p. 4.

interlacing ornament, formed of the convolutions of the bodies of two, or probably of four winged serpents. This also was found buried in the church-yard of St. Denis.

No. 8. One half of a large tombstone of the full length of the grave, ornamented with rude scrolls and battlemented work. Found in the wall of the church of St. Mary, Bishophill, Junior.—*The Rev. C. J. Buncombe, Vicar,* 1861.

No. 9. A portion of the shaft of a cross, ornamented with scroll-work and figures in high relief. Found during the restoration of the church of St. Mary, Bishophill, Junior.*— *Purchased,* 1877. '

No. 10. A portion of the head of a fine cross of late Saxon work, probably of the eleventh century, discovered whilst rebuilding the church of St. Mary, Castlegate.†—*The Rector and Churchwardens,* 1871.

No. 11. The base of a cross, rudely and curiously ornamented; also the head of another cross (perhaps the same) found under the city wall, in the archway leading from the Old Station to the New.—*The Directors, N.E. Railway,* 1874.

No. 12. The centre of a cross-head, which has been painted red. On one side is an ornamental flower; on the other, the following inscription in very early characters, the whole forming a pentameter line, applicable, probably, to our Blessed Lord. There have been inscriptions also on the arms of the cross :

> SALVE P
> RO MERITIS
> PRS ALME
> TVIS.

i.e., Salve pro meritis, presbyter alme, Tuis.—Probably found at York.

---

* A coffin-lid of the Saxon period is built into the wall of the neighbouring church of St. Mary, Bishophill, Senior, where it is going slowly to decay.

† The dedication stone ¦was found at the same time and is carefully preserved. See Report for 1870, p. 53, where a photograph of this curious stone is given.

No. 13. A very interesting fragment of an early Saxon cross, found some years ago at Ripon, near the site of the old monastery. It is inscribed

+ ADHVSE
PR̄B

i.e., *Adhuse presbyter*, a name which occurs in the Liber Vitæ of Durham cathedral.—*Purchased of Mr. Sharpin of Ripon*, 1872.

No. 14. The shaft and a portion of the head of a large cross, more than 5ft. high, richly ornamented with scroll-work on three sides. It was discovered at Wakefield, constituting the step to a barber's shop, by the feet of whose customers the sculpture on the fourth side has been completely worn down.—*Obtained for the Society in* 1870 *by Mr. Fairless Barber.*

No. 15. A small coped tombstone of a child, with a cross under the end or gable ; also a part of one of the arms of a cross, with interlacing work. Found at Ingleby Arncliffe.— *Rev. R. J. Steele, Vicar of Ingleby*, 1879.

No. 16. The original font of the church of Hutton Cranswick, discarded at the recent restoration of the church, and recovered from a rockery and reconstructed. It seems to be of early eleventh century work. Around the font in ten panels is a series of subjects, among which are bell-ringing, wrestling, shooting with the bow, the Holy Lamb, the Tree of Life, and several uncouth figures. This font resembles that at Belton in Lincolnshire.—*Rev. C. D. Pudsey, Vicar of Hutton Cranswick*, 1880.

III. Anglo-Norman.

Under this head are comprised some specimens of the architecture which prevailed in this country from the Conquest to the end of the 12th century. The greater part of them are remains of the first Abbey of St. Mary. In the churches of York and its neighbourhood, as well as in the crypt of the Minster, this style of architecture is richly exemplified.

No. 1. Capitals, gurgoyles, and other remains of the abbey erected by Stephen, the first abbat, in the reign of William Rufus.*

No. 2. Sculptured stones discovered in the foundations of a house in Micklegate, and probably belonging to the Priory church of the Holy Trinity, near which they were found. Among them is a stone representing the Flight into Egypt.— *Mr. Pulleyn.*

No. 3. A curious sculpture which must originally have occupied the tympanum of a door, representing the soul leaving the body of a dying man, and being seized by evil spirits. It was found reversed in the dungeon of a building near the N.W. tower of the Minster.—*Deposited by the Dean and Chapter,* 1862.

No. 4. The remains of a fine Norman door from St. Mary's Abbey, with a double dog-tooth moulding, boldly and finely cut.

No. 5. A portion of a very fine and lofty arch of Norman work from the same place.

No. 6. A portion of the arch of the door-way at the entrance to St. William's Chapel, which stood at the south-west end of the old bridge over the Ouse, and was removed preparatory to the erection of the new bridge, in 1810. There is a fine engraving of this door-way in Halfpenny's Fragmenta Vetusta.

No. 7. A single arch of the arcade inside the same chapel, fixed to the wall in a position similar to that which it originally occupied; upon it is laid a single stone of the richly-

---

* It must be understood that the sculptured stones to which no different locality is assigned were found among the ruins of St. Mary's Abbey.

carved string-course which ran above. The arcade is drawn and etched in Cave's Antiquities of York.

No. 8. Several Norman fragments taken out of the wall of the Will Office at the restoration of the South Transept of the Minster, and probably a portion of the choir which was built by Archbishop Roger (A.D. 1154—1181).—*Dean and Chapter of York*, 1877.

No. 9. An imperfect arch of Transitional work which formed a part of the beautiful chapter-house of St. Mary's Abbey. It can scarcely have belonged to the pier which still remains in its original position, but, wherever it stood, it has the honor of having been regarded by the late Sir Gilbert Scott* as the noblest doorway in England. The remains on the floor, under the arch, are all of similar work, and probably belonged to the chapter-house.

No. 10. Appended to the wall is the west window of the old church of St. Maurice,† York, of Transitional work. It is one of the earliest approaches to tracery, and is of two lights, round-headed, with a plain, small circle over them in the head. It is engraved by Mr. J. H. Parker, in his Architectural Notes on the York Churches.—*The Rector and Churchwardens of St. Maurice*, 1875.

No. 11. A portion of an arch of Transitional work found in St. Leonard's Place, and no doubt a part of the buildings of St. Leonard's Hospital. The remainining portion of this arch is alluded to on page 14.—*The City Commissioners*, 1835.

No. 12. Capital of a pillar of Transitional work found in Gillygate.—*Mr. G. Bell*, 1872.

---

* See a paper, with drawings, by him in the Transactions of the Institute of British Architects.

† The Norman door of this church, which bore traces of colour when found, is set up in the gardens of the late Mr. Joseph Buckle, in Monkgate.

IV. EARLY ENGLISH, DECORATED, AND PERPENDICULAR.

Under this head come the remaining specimens of Mediæval sculpture, which the Society possesses. The greater part of them, it will be seen, belonged to St. Mary's Abbey, and were wrought in the grounds now occupied by these gardens, in which they have always continued, being parts of the church which was built by Abbat Simon de Warwick, in the latter half of the thirteenth century.

The Visitor will observe an endless variety of Early English and Decorated sculpture in beautiful profusion. There is so much that it is impossible to give a minute description of it. We may mention however :

No. 1. Several portions of a noble door-way, in which the hollow of the arch has been ornamented by groups of figures in high relief and exquisitely sculptured.

No. 2. The greater part of a grand capital of richly clustering foliage, from the entrance to the vestibule of the Chapter-house from the Cloister.

No. 3. A number of beautiful bosses, of a very large size, from a room marked F. in the Ground-plan. One of these (a) represents the Holy Lamb surrounded by maple leaves, a staple and ring being still inserted in the stone from which a lamp was originally suspended. b. Another large boss represents the Virgin Mary in the midst of vine-branches. c. A third shows a monk playing on an instrument resembling the modern violin.

No. 4. A fine series of thirteen smaller bosses, some from the room F., others from different parts of the abbey, as shown by Mr. Wellbeloved in his Account of the Excavations. They consist of representations of leaves and animals.

No. 5. Fragments of two large figures representing the coronation of the Blessed Virgin.

No. 6. A specimen of the lower walling and of the buttresses in the Cloister, removed from its place on the north-east side of the cloister, near the vestibule of the Chapter-house.

No. 7. A large mutilated figure of the Virgin and Child.

No. 8. Another imperfect statue of Maria Salome, the wife of Zebedee, and mother of SS. James and John.

No. 9. A small mutilated effigy in chain armour, with a surcoat, found near the site of the innermost of the walls of the Abbey, between the Hospitium and the river. It has stood, no doubt, on the outside of a gateway, upon the battlement, as may still be seen at Alnwick castle.

No. 10. Ten Statues fixed against the pillars of the room. These statues are a portion of a series which, it is probable, adorned the Triforium of the Abbey Church built by Simon de Warwick. They were discovered in the south aisle of the nave of the church, at the depth of about 8ft., lying with the faces downward, under a mass of stones composed chiefly of the tracery-work of the windows of the church, cemented together with the mortar used in building the palace of Henry VIII. (See p. 22.) The drapery of all had been painted and gilded; but the colours and the gilding soon faded upon being exposed to the light and air. Of these statues, so carefully concealed by some one whose good taste and feeling had not been overpowered by religious zeal, three are manifestly designed to represent aged Jews; the remaining four, supposing those which are headless to have been similar to those which are perfect, have nothing of a Jewish character, and are youthful in their appearance. Of how many statues, the series, when complete, consisted, cannot now be known. Some may have been wantonly destroyed; some were certainly carried away. One of these having long formed part of the arch of the bridge at Clifton, has been restored,* in a sadly

* By the Overseers of Clifton in 1839.

weather-worn state, to its fellows ; and two others, undoubtedly belonging to the series, after having long served as coping-stones to the wall of the church-yard of St. Lawrence, without Walmgate Bar,* and having been subsequently fixed on each side of the north doorway, have also been placed in the Museum. Such a series must have had some meaning, historical, legendary, or emblematical. Imperfect as the series is, enough, perhaps, is left to indicate what it may have been designed to represent. Of the three Jewish figures, one is evidently the representation of Moses. It bears his usual emblems—the two tables of stone, the rod with the serpent, and the horns on forehead.† The two other Jewish figures have nothing to fix their designation.‡ Of the two figures removed from the church-yard of St. Lawrence, one is that of St. John the Baptist, with his distinguishing emblem, the Holy Lamb, on his arm. Supposing that there were originally no more than three Jewish figures in the series, the intro-duction of St. John the Baptist appears to offer the clue to the interpretation of the whole. Moses may be supposed to be emblematical of " the Law ; " the two other Jewish figures may represent " the Prophets ; " the more youthful figures, " the Apostles or preachers of the Gospel," the newer or younger dispensation. The statue of the Baptist being placed between these and the former, the whole series would artisti-

* Given in 1838.

† The sculptor, either following preceding artists, or misled by understanding literally the figurative epithet "flying," given to the fiery serpent by the prophet Isaiah, has added to the serpent in the hand of Moses the body and wings of a bird. In making Moses appear horned, he has followed the Vulgate Latin Version of Exod. xxxiv. 30; where, instead of "the face of Moses shone," as in our authorised version, the Vulgate has, "videntes cornutam Moysi faciem," seeing that the face of Moses was horned.

‡ Perhaps the red colour of the drapery of the second of these figures may indi-cate Elijah, the most eminent of the prophets, and his translation in a chariot of fire, 2 Kings, ii. 16. As the forerunner of the Messiah, his statue would appro-priately precede the Baptist and the Christian series.—[J. K.]

cally represent the words of our Lord, as recorded by the Evangelist Luke : " The Law and the Prophets were until John ; since that time the kingdom of God is preached."— Ch. xvi. 16.

No. 11. Bases and pillars of Petworth or Purbeck marble, with several other sculptured stones from the South Transept of the Minster, erected by Archbishop Gray, circa 1240. Among them is the only original capital that was found on the South front.—*The Dean and Chapter of York*, 1876.

No. 12. A number of beautiful sculptures in Derbyshire marble, in Perpendicular work, which have originally formed part of a series of stalls. They may, perhaps, have been taken from St. Sepulchre's chapel, or from some other part of the Minster, probably from the former place. They have been found on several occasions " inclosed between two walls in a private house," or otherwise concealed, as if there was at least the hope that they might be again utilized if a change in religion should be made. They found their way to various parts of the city, having been, as Thoresby says, " sold by parcels to statuaries, and others, for common use." Many of these sculptures are now collected in the Museum, and others may still be seen in gardens and walls in the city. The greater part of these sculptures which the Society possesses were found in Precentor's Court, in 1835, and were presented to the Museum in 1835 and 1861, by Mr. and Mrs. Swineard, on whose premises they were found. Another portion, removed from the North-east side of Clifford's Tower, to which it had long been affixed, was given by the High Sheriff and Magistrates of the county ; a third piece, showing the sculpture between the niches and the cornice, from the garden of Mr. Robert Driffield, on the Mount, was presented by Mr. Wm. Driffield, in 1853. The head of a stall found buried in a cellar in Lawrence Street, and deposited for some time in St.

Lawrence church-yard, was given in 1876, by the Rev. George Wade, Vicar of St. Lawrence, York.*

No, 13. A portion of a fine door-way, beautifully wrought. Two figures are represented as attending an aged person. This sculpture was found in Mr. Swineard's house, but it is of an earlier date than the carving which has just been described.

No. 14. Several very fine and delicately carved fragments of the same date as the door-way with which they were found. They are parts of stalls and canopies.

No. 15. A finely wrought shield, slung in the centre of a quatrefoil, and found near the Guildhall.—*Purchased*, 1878.

No. 16. A bracket (appended to the wall) supported on the shoulders of an angel, found in a house in High Petergate. *Mr. W. D. Lund*, 1879.

No. 17. A cast from a crucifix, which was found, some years ago, in the ruins of a small chapel dedicated to St Mary, on the south-east side of Sherburn Church.† On one side are figures of the Saviour, the Virgin, and St. John ; on medallions, at the ends of the transverse limb, are the sword and the lantern, and the purse or bag of money ; and on a shield at the end of the upright limb, the seamless coat and the dice.   On the other side are the same figures ; and on the corresponding medallions and shield are the reed and the sponge, the hammer, nails, and pincers ; the heart, the hands, and the feet.   On one extremity of the transverse limb is a rude representation of an ear.   The date of the original is supposed to be towards the end of the fifteenth century.   The recent history of the original is remarkable.   Upon being discovered, it was taken by the churchwarden to adorn the

* *cf.* Thoresby's Ducatus Leodiensis, 2nd ed., app. 115; Hunter's Account of Henry the Eighth's progress in Yorkshire; Browne's York Minster, i. 132-3; Cave's Antiquities of York, plate 36.

† Engraved in Whitaker's Loidis and Elmete, p. 150, and in Brayley's Graphic Illustrator, p. 136.

Hall of Steeton, near Sherburn, where he resided. This act was resented by the parishioners; and, after much contention, it was agreed that the stone should be divided between the Hall and the church. Accordingly it was sawn vertically into two equal portions; one of which was retained at the Hall, and the other—the portion first described above—was restored to the church, where it may now be seen.—*Mr. G. Fowler Jones,* 1846.

No. 18. A large holy-water stoup, from St. Mary's Abbey. It is placed close to the entrance door.

No. 19. A small and prettily-ornamented holy-water stoup, found at Whorlton, in Cleveland.—*Rev. J. W. Darnbrough, Vicar of South Otterington,* 1872.

No. 20. A stone, with a plain cross in relief, brought from the Castle Mills, destroyed in 1856. These mills originally belonged to the Knights Templar. The chapel, over the doorway of which this stone was placed, belonged to the Guild of St. George.—*The Corporation of York,* 1856.

No. 21. Two stones, from the ruins of the Abbey, in which holes, round or otherwise, are cut. Some similar objects have been recently engraved in the Transactions of the Cumberland and Westmerland Antiquarian Society. From the "Rites of Durham," we learn that 'in either end of the Dorter (Domitory), was a four-square stone, wherein was a dozen cressets wrought, being ever filled and supplied by the cooke as they needed, to give light to the monks and novices, when they rose to theire mattins at midnight, and for their other necessarye uses.'

No. 22. Three fragments of terra-cotta moulding found among the ruins of the Abbey.

No. 23. Part of a gravestone with DE : HARPHAM upon it in early letters. A Robert de Harpham was abbat between 1184 and 1189, and another member of his family was a benefactor to the house.

E

No. 24. The greater part of a coffin lid, charged with a cross, and inscribed :

HIC JACET EMMA DE BEN . . . .

Emma de Benfield, widow of Adam de Benfield of Marton-in-Cleveland, was a benefactress to the Abbey of St. Mary, and, in token of gratitude, was no doubt interred in the church in which her monument was found. The stone is probably of the latter half of the 13th century.

No. 25. A large portion of a marble slab, bearing the matrix of a brass, which probably commemorated some abbat towards the close of the 13th century.

No. 26. Part of a marble coffin-lid, with the beginning of an inscription, HIC JACET, etc., in noble letters from 7 to 11in. high. From the Abbey.

No. 27. An imperfect sepulchral slab, showing part of an incised cross, and the following remains of an inscription in letters filled with lead :

ME · RE : GIST : ICI : ANNAIS : FV : LA FILGE : PERIS . . .

This stone was found among the ruins of the Abbey.

No. 28. A large portion of an early coffin-lid, used as a walling-stone in the church of St. Helen, bearing a cross with the following inscription on the edge : + ANNAIS : DE : GRANTHAM : GIST : ICI : DEV :—the remainder contained the usual petition for mercy. A William de Grantham founded a chantry in St. Helen's in 1371.—*Mr. Robert Weatherley*, 1878.

No. 29. A large and fine monumental effigy in chain-armour, which served as a boundary mark of the parish of St. Margaret, in Walmgate ; being half-buried in the ground against a wall on the east side of Newtgate. The arms on the shield are those of the family of Vescy, and as the shield has a bar sinister across it, we have probably the monument of a rather celebrated personage in his day, Sir John de Vescy, illegitimate son of William de Vescy, lord of Alnwick, who died in the beginning of the 14th century, to which period this figure belongs. On the widening of Newtgate (now called St. George's Street) this effigy was removed.—*The City Com-missioners.*

No. 30. A mutilated effigy, which during a long period was placed, with the lower half buried in the ground, at the end of the village of Clifton, near York, by the side of the turnpike road leading to Easingwold. It is too much defaced to afford the slightest indication of the knight it was intended to represent. This figure used popularly to be called " Mother Shipton's " stone, from the tradition that she was burnt to death by its side.—*Mr. David Russell*, 1851.

No. 31. Part of a coffin-lid, 14th century, from the floor of the church of St. Mary, Bishophill, Junior, bearing the head of a cross flory.—*Rev. C. J. Buncombe*, 1861.

No. 32. A sepulchral slab found buried in the church-yard of St. Denis, bearing a cross flory. On one side of the shaft is a three-legged melting-pot or caldron, on the other a bell, showing that the person commemorated had been a bell-founder.—*Purchased*, 1848.

No. 33. The heads of two coffin-lids bearing incised crosses, from the church-yard of St. Denis.—*Purchased*, 1848.

No. 34. The greater part of the head of an incised cross found under the Bonded Warehouse in Skeldergate.—*Pur-chased*, 1880.

No. 35. The greater part of a coffin-lid bearing a plain cross, found in York.—*Rev. George Rowe*, 1881.

No. 36. This large sepulchral slab was found at the western end of the Hospitium, amongst the foundations of some buildings, of a date later than the dissolution of the Abbey, from the church or cloister of which it had probably been removed. It bears an incised cross flory, and an inscription in the writing characteristic of the beginning of the fifteenth century, which may be read thus :

*Hic jacent frates Willielmus magister et dominus Johannes Hewyk capellanus, quondam filii Johannis et Agnetis Hewyk.**

Beneath the inscription appear the incised outlines, now nearly obliterated, of the bust of these brothers, one on each side of the shaft of the cross, with their hands raised on the breast in the attitude of devotion.

No. 37. Part of the tomb of Archbishop Rotherham, who died in the year 1500, erected on the north side of the Lady Chapel, in the Minster, and nearly destroyed in the fire of 1829.—*Deposited by the Dean and Chapter of York*, 1862.

No. 38. Numerous fragments of sepulchral slabs, chiefly of a late date, found among the ruins of the Abbey, too imperfect to indicate of whom they were the memorials.

No. 39. Portions of a sculptured monument removed from the City Wall, near Fishergate Bar, commemorating the repair of sixty yards of the wall in the mayoralty of Sir William Tod, knight, in 1487.—*Mr. Robert Sunter*, 1858.

No. 40. A tablet which had been built into the wall of the house which formerly stood at the corner of St. Saviourgate and Colliergate, bearing the following inscription :

" *Here stood the image of Yorke and remeved* [removed] †
in the year of our Lord God, A.M.VC.I. (1501), *unto the Common Hall in the time of the mairalty of John Stockdale.*"

The image is supposed to have been that of Ebraucus, whom Geoffrey of Monmouth imagined to have been the founder of York. In 1738 a restored figure of Ebraucus was ordered to be fixed in a niche in Bootham Bar.—*Mr. Oswald Allen*, 1839.

* A family of some note of the name of Hewyk was at that time settled in Cleveland. See Test. Ebor. ii. p. 247.

† "He hath *remeved* the sottie
Of that unwise fantaisie." Gower Conf. Am. Lib. 8.

No. 41. Fragments of a stone inscribed in large letters, CIVITATI, which stood in the old entrance to York castle from Castlegate, and marked the limits of the jurisdiction of the city. Given to the Dean and Chapter by Mr. George Todd.— *Deposited by the Dean and Chapter*, 1862.

III.

ANTIQUITIES IN THE UPPER ROOM OF THE HOSPITIUM.

With the exception of a long case filled with mediæval and more recent pottery and tiles, this room is now entirely devoted to Roman remains which have been discovered in York.

I. ROMAN.

A.

No. 1. The centre of the room is occupied by two Roman tessellated pavements. The largest of these was removed in 1857, by permission of Sir George Wombwell, from his estate at Oulston, near Easingwold. Its present length is 23ft., but it had originally extended to 36ft., and had evidently been the floor of a corridor in a Roman villa. Its most remarkable peculiarity is the semicircular apse, originally raised between seven and eight inches above the level of the pavement, and containing the figure of a vase within a labyrinth border. It is not improbable that it supported a statue, or a bust, as it appears to have stood near the entrance. Nothing was discovered by which the age of the pavement could be ascertained.

No. 2.   The same enclosed space contains a portion of the Roman pavement which was discovered in 1854, on an estate at Dalton Parlours, near Collingham, belonging to Lady Betty Hastings' Charity, and was removed thence by permission of her trustees.*   It is a part of a semicircular termination of an apartment in a Roman villa, occupied, it is probable, by an officer of the Sixth Legion, its stamp having been found on one of the tiles of the hypocaust.   The head is that of Medusa, or a Gorgon.

No. 3.   A portion of a tessellated pavement, 5ft. 6in. square, found in Tanner Row in 1846, a few yards above the entrance to Barker Lane, in excavating for the York and North Midland Railway.   The remaining portion is probably still buried beneath the street.   The figure represented in the design is that of an imaginary sea monster, having the head and forelegs of a bull, and the body and tail of a fish.   Above, on the wall, is a coloured sketch of the pavement prepared for the late Mr. Hargrove.—*From Mr. Hargrove's Collection*, 1847.

No. 4.   A portion of the border of a large pavement, originally 18 feet square, found on Toft Green in 1853.   Some other pieces of it are in the basement story of the Museum.

No. 5.   One of the corners of a third pavement discovered at the same time and place.   A coloured drawing of this pavement, as it was found, hangs against the wall, and some other portions are in the basement story of the Museum.

No. 6.   Another pavement was discoved in 1881, on Cherry Hill, in Clementhorpe, and for one reason or another is still in the ground, although promised to the Society.   A portion of it only, 11ft. by 8ft., was uncovered.   There is a description of the pavement in the *York Herald* for the time, and a

---

* See a paper by Dr. Procter, in the Proceedings of the Yorkshire Philosophical Society, p. 270, Pl. 7, where a position of the Pavement is represented, which it was impossible to remove.

drawing of it was made by Mr. Plows. In one angle was a heart, in another a tulip or a bell. The pavement had been much injured.

No. 7. Some fragments of a very fine pavement, the remainder of which still lies under the rampart of the city wall, close to Micklegate Bar, are preserved in the basement of the Museum. It was found in 1814. The pavement had been ruined by curiosity-hunters before any attempt was made to take it up. Happily, a beautifully coloured drawing of it was made by Mr. Fowler, of Winterton, a copy of which is appended to the wall at the upper end of the room. From it the design of the original may be pretty accurately made out.

The recent restoration of the church of St. Mary, in Castle-gate, showed that the buttress on the left side of the entrance door was resting upon a Roman pavement, the greater part of which must necessarily have been destroyed. A careful rubbing of it was made on which the colours were inserted, and this is in the possession of the Society.

There is also a fine pavement in the village of Acomb, near York, of which some fragments are in the Museum; and several others are known to exist. But the Curator prefers to keep this knowledge to himself until due provision can be made for their removal. To disclose the secret would only result in their inevitable destruction.

At the upper part of the room is a series of drawings of the already known Yorkshire pavements, including those at Hovingham and Aldborough. Among those of the latter place is an original sketch of a pavement which does not correspond with any existing remains.

CASE B.

A noble collection of several hundred specimens of Romano-British ware, the work of Roman potters settled in Britain, and discovered at York. Vestiges of Roman potteries have been traced at Middlethorpe, Castle Howard, and Holme-on-Spalding-Moor. There is every reason to believe that much of the pottery in this Museum was made at York itself, and the time has arrived when a new nomenclature for the various wares might be advantageously adopted. Undoubted remains of kilns have been discovered in Staffordshire, in the district to which, in modern times, science and art have given such just celebrity ; in Oxfordshire, also, and in various other parts of Britain. But the most extensive and remarkable remains of Roman potteries have been found in Northamptonshire, in the neighbourhood of the ancient Roman station Durobrivæ (now Caistor, near Peterborough.) On the banks of the Nen and its tributaries, the late Mr. Artis traced, through the extent of twenty miles, the kilns and works of Roman potters, in which he computed that no less than 2000 hands may have been employed. Similar works have been discovered on the banks and along the creeks of the Medway, and in other parts of Kent. On the top of this case are the remains of four large *amphoræ*, two of which are nearly perfect. One of these has been cut in two, and has been used, probably for sepulchral purposes. The smallest of the four was found at Kertch, in the Crimea, and was brought from the Museum there by the Rev. J. J. Harrison, and presented to this Society. Some notice of this curious class of vessels will be given subsequently.

I—II. B. Cinerary urns of various shapes and sizes. When found, they contained fragments of bones and ashes. The bluish-black colour of these vessels is not the natural colour of the clay, but the effect of their being baked in what Mr. Artis denominated " smother-kilns," kilns so constructed that the fire was suffocated by the smoke of vegetable substances, when the contents of the kiln had acquired a sufficient degree of heat to insure uniformity of colour. In some instances vessels have been discovered in the York Cemeteries which have been artificially coloured to make them suitable for their melancholy office.

On the tops of the Cases in the room, a large number of Cinerary urns of various sizes and colours are arranged. Lids of pot have been sometimes found with them. Some of these may be seen in Case H.

III—IV—V. B. Smaller vessels of dark clay of various shapes and sizes. The greater part have been found in graves, having been placed there with food or liquid for the use of the deceased.

In IV. B. is a vessel, marked *a*, which was found at Boston, on the Wharfe, about three miles from Tadcaster (the Roman station Calcaria), in the year 1848, in digging for the foundation of a house. It contained Roman silver coins, many of them belonging to the Consular and Family series, much worn; the rest to the series of Imperial denarii; the latest being coins of Hadrian, during whose reign, it is probable, the treasure was concealed. The coins of Nerva, Trajan, and Hadrian are in excellent preservation.* The whole find, consisting of 172 coins, was purchased by the Society in 1880.

VI. B. A series of jugs of various shapes and colours, including three *gutturnia*, and examples of other rare forms. The *gutturnium* had its mouth compressed, so as to lessen the stream which flowed from the interior.

VII. B. On this shelf are several double-handled *ampullæ*, two or three of which were probably carried by means of a cord slung through the handles.

* *cf.* Journal Arch. Assn., v. 89. The Museum possesses a careful catalogue of these coins, drawn up by Mr. Wellbeloved.

E 2

a. A fine vessel, found in 1876, when excavating for the New Railway Station.

b. A smaller vessel of the same character, found, with numerous fragments of pottery, at Scoreby, near York, on the bank of the Derwent, between Kexby and Stamford Bridge, not far, perhaps, from a Roman post or station.—*Mr. John Wood*, 1847.

c. A large vessel, with a cover of red ware, found in 1872 on the site of the depôts for the New Railway Station. It was filled with fragments of bones. When softened with warm water to allow them to be removed, a fragrant smell was perceptible, arising from the pungent oils with which the bones had been originally drenched. Some particles of glutinous matter, like gum, were detached from them.

VIII. B. Several vessels of a singular pattern, called by Mr. Thomas Wright, the " frilled pattern," supposed to be formed " by moulding thin *laminæ* of clay on a previously formed vase."* As vessels of this description have not been found at any of the Southern or Northern stations in Britain, or in the extensive kilns of Northamptonshire or Kent, it has been conjectured that they were exclusively manufactured in the potteries of Eburacum.

IX. B. Vessels of variously coloured clays, with slightly indented patterns on the sides. Several of them have been coloured black for funereal purposes. This colour can be easily washed off.

In the centre is a beautiful vase with arms, made evidently after a Greek model, but in a coarse clay. It was found in 1872, under the Railway bridge at the entrance into the New Station. Near it are several vessels of pale red ware, ornamented with white. Among them is a vessel of white ware,

---

* Rivers, Mountains, and Sea Coasts of Yorkshire, by J. Phillips, F.R.S., p. 290.
Two of these vessels are figured in Meteyard's Life of Josiah Wedgwood, i. 13.

so delicately thin as to resemble almost the modern egg shell china, but lacking its transparency. It was discovered during the Railway excavations of 1872.

X. B. On the shelves are some vessels of dark clay, ornamented with white lines or scrolls. Two of them have the following inscriptions running around them :

MI : CEMI
AXSASI

Below, in the centre, is a fine two-handled vessel of pale red ware, with several remarkable specimens of pottery near. Among these are two triplets of urns linked together, such as are still in use for flowers.

At the sides are a number of vessels of white clay, ornamented with red lines and patterns.

XI. B. A number of bottles of dark clay. In the centre is a two-handled *ampulla* found on the Mount, and remarkable for having a double frill running round the neck.

XII. B. Some urns and an *ampulla* of red ware. Also several handsome vessels of dark clay, with fluted hollows in their sides, which were formed when the vessel was in a pliable state, soon after its removal from the lathe. Mr. Artis found a quantity of this pottery in the course of his excavations in Northamptonshire.

XIII. B. A large collection of these fluted vessels, some of great beauty in colour and form.

XIV. B. A number of fine vessels with ornaments in relief, some representing hunting scenes, another pease stalks and flowers, and others, twisted scroll-work.

The hunting subjects were laid on, according to Mr. Artis, by means of sharp and blunt skewer-instruments after the vessel had been thrown on the wheel : the vessel was then dipped in the glaze, and placed in the kiln. Vessels of this description appear to have been manufactured very extensively in the potteries of the Durobrivian district.

XV. B.   A quantity of exquisitely shaped vessels with a glaze of shining black.   One of these, (*a*) a beautiful *ampulla*, was found during the recent Railway excavations.   In a portion of a similar vessel, (*b*) were found in the year 1840, on the site of the house erected for the residence of the secretary of the North Eastern Railway, upwards of 200 * Roman silver coins, now in the possession of the Yorkshire Philosophical Society.   Five of them are of the Consular or Family series, much worn and illegible ; eighteen are denarii of some of the early emperors ; the rest range from Septimius Severus to M. Jul. Philippus.   Many belonging to the later emperor appear to have been cast in moulds, and not to have been in circulation.—*The Hargrove Collection.*

XVI. B.   A large collection of small finger cups of various colours and sizes, principally, no doubt, intended for unguents and perfumes, and the usual accompaniments of a lady's toilet table.

The three little red cups were found during the Railway excavations in 1872, and retained traces of some glutinous substance.

XVII. B.   A number of jugs, red and black.

CASE C.

This case contains most of the specimens of Roman glass which the Museum possesses.

Few glass vessels in an entire state have been found in York ; but fragments of such vessels have frequently been met with.   A collection of these serves to show the state of

---

* Another find of about 200 denarii was made near the Foss Islands about 1868, but the coins were unhappily dispersed.   The number 200 would appear to have been a *numerus receptus.*

perfection which the manufacture of glass had attained in ancient times, and the taste and skill of the artists engaged in it. Few vestiges of Roman glass-works have been traced in Britain; it is probable, therefore, that most of the glass -vessels discovered in Roman stations and burial places in this country were imported from Gaul, where, as we learn from Pliny, such vessels were fabricated in his time.

ON THE STAND IN THE CENTRE OF THE CASE.

a. Several minute bottles about 1in. in height.

b. Two small bottles of white glass, and two other vessels of the same material, and nearly of the same size, which were placed, inverted, on the top of the former, found together with a cinerary urn, or *ossuarium*, of lead (in case M) in a lead coffin in 1840. They probably contained unguents, balsam, or some other funeral offerings.*—*From Mr. Hargrove's Collection*, 1847.

c. Two large unguent bottles, out of a number found under a tomb of tiles, which bore the mark of the Sixth Legion, under the new Railway Station in 1873. These vessels used to be called lachrymatories, from the idle fancy that they held the tears of the mourners at the funeral.—*The Directors, N.E. Railway*, 1873.

d. A small bottle, slightly imperfect, with miniature handles.—*The Directors, N.E. Railway*, 1874.

e. The greater part of a bowl, like a modern finger-glass, with an incised pattern.

f. Two small vessels, one an unguent bottle, the other a cup with fluted sides, found in a stone coffin,—*The Cook Collection*, 1872.

g. A choice jug of bluish-green glass, found with a black vase in a stone coffin at Clementhorpe.—*Mr J. Braddock*, 1863.

* For an account of this find, with engravings of the glass and the ossuarium, *cf*, Coll. Antiqua, vii., pp. 174—6.

h. A very prettily shaped bottle, on a stand, found with a bronze lamp.—*The Directors, N.E. Railway,* 1874.

i. Several conical pieces of glass, hollowed, one of them ornamented with two small beaded studs of blue glass, which seem to have been appended to the sides of vases.

j. The neck of a vessel of white glass ornamented with a spiral cord of fine blue. Found on Toft Green.—*Purchased.*

k. A vessel shaped like a modern tumbler, from a stone coffin on the Mount.—*The Cook Collection,* 1872.

l. A number of small unguent bottles. On the base of one of them (from the Cook Collection) is the maker's name PATRI. M.

ON THE FLOOR OF THE CASE.

a. A large jug, 12in. high, much injured, around which are arranged fragments of other jugs, etc.

b. A similar vessel found in a barrow near Wharram-le-Street in 1820.—*Rev. E. W. Stillingfleet,* 1865.

c. A fine unguent bottle, 15in. long, set in a stand. From the recent Railway excavations, 1874.

d. A vessel with a broken rim, with a beautiful patina on it, found in a stone coffin on the site of the New Railway Station, close to the face of a female.—*The Directors N.E. Railway,* 1873.

e. Studs and portions of pins of glass.* The head of one of these is in the shape of a white bird, the wings being tipped with blue. This was found under the City Wall in 1872.

f. Roundlets of coloured glass, probably, to set in brooches. From the Railway excavations, 1874—5.

g. A large number of beads of various sizes and colours.†

---

* See Journal Arch. Inst., xxii. 386, for a notice of some glass pins found at Dorchester.

† See Journal Arch. Inst. viii. 351, etc., for a Paper by Prof. Buckman, on the Composition of British and Roman beads.

h. A small ring of green glass, ornamented with blue and white lines. Found in an urn during the Railway excavations in 1873. A larger one of dark blue, striped with white and purple, found in Holgate Lane in 1878. Fragments of others.

i. Fragments of richly coloured vessels.

j. Pieces of pillared* glass bowls, green and dark blue in colour, found under the Exhibition building in 1878.

k. A number of partially fused unguent bottles, found in an urn, under the War Offices in Fishergate, in 1876, having been taken with the ashes from the funeral pyre.

l. Two bottles, similarly fused, from the recent Railway excavations.

m. The contents of the trinket box of a Roman lady, which was interred with her, found in 1874 under the new Railway Station. They consist, with the tire and lock of the box, of four large jet bracelets, three jet pins, and two curious glass vessels, one of which is in the shape of a hollow ring.— *Exhibited by Mr. Cartell.*

n. The contents of a similar box, found during the Railway excavations, in 1873, laid under the back of a skeleton, which was found by the side of a stone coffin (See p. 25).

In the box were at least six glass vessels and a large silver ring. The brass tire of the box is remarkably fine.

o. A fine unguent bottle, with fluted sides, from the R.E. of 1872†—*Exhibited by Mr. F. Bean.*

p. Fragments of coarse window glass.

q. A number of handles of vessels, some exceedingly fine.

r. Bases of vessels, rounded off by Roman children to play with.

s. Fragments of vessels, principally of cut-glass, some of which must have been of great beauty. One of them is a

---

* *cf.* Isca Silurum, ed. 1862, plate xxvii. and C. R. Smith's London, pp. 121—3.

† It is exactly similar to one found near Bath in 1840, and now at Alnwick. *Aquæ Solis,* pl. xlv.

fragment of a small bluish-green glass vase, on the rim of which has been represented a chariot race in the Circus. On this portion of the rim is seen a *quadriga* with the charioteer, and part of the fore-legs of the horses of another *quadriga* following; and between these the column bearing the seven *ora*, by means of which the spectators could count the number of rounds in the course which had been run; one of the *ova* being taken down at the completion of each course.†

Under Case C, is a small lead coffin, found during the R.E. circa 1840.

CASE D.

This, and the next case, contain vessels and numerous fragments of the beautiful fictile ware, usually called SAMIAN, from the Greek island Samos, where a manufactory of such ware was established at a very early period. It is distinguished by its compact texture, and its red or coral-colour glaze. It was held in great esteem by the Romans, and extensively used by them at table, and for other domestic purposes. The manufactory of such ware was not confined to Samos. It extended to Italy, Spain, and Gaul,—whence, it is probable, —and specially from Gaul,—it was imported into Britain. It was made also in the potteries in this country, although probably of an inferior class. A portion of a mould for making Samian vessels has been found in York. There is a ware still made at Talavera, and other places in Spain, which is very similar to Samian.

Vessels of this ware are of two kinds, embossed and plain. The former are commonly in the shape of bowls, or drinking cups, of various sizes. They are generally ornamented with a festoon and tassel-border, and, below that, with elegant scrolls of foliage, flowers, and fruit, or with a variety of

† See Dict. Gr.[and Rom. Antiq. CIRCUS . . C. R. Smith's London, p. 121; and Cat. o. his Museum, p. 48.

designs, representing divinities and their emblems, sacrificial ceremonies, bacchanalian processions, gladiatorial combats, the chase of wild animals (*venatio*,)—which formed part of the sports of the arena,—and other subjects connected with ancient customs.

The plain or unembossed vessels of this ware are generally of a smaller size, and of a great variety of form. Some are ornamented with a simple ivy-leaf scroll on the rim; and others with a pattern, resembling the engine-turned work of modern watch cases.

I. D. *a.* The greater part of a bowl, nearly 9in. in diameter, ornamented with lions, boars, wolves, etc. From the recent Railway excavations.*—*Mr. F. Leak*, 1872.

b. A bowl, nearly perfect, 7in. in diameter, of coarse ware, showing a mending of lead. It was found at Clifton, and is ornamented with figures and stags' heads.—*Mr. J. F. Walker*, 1872.

c. A small, very coarse, and English-made bowl, 7½in. in diameter, adorned with deer and dogs. It was found in Priory Street.—*Purchased*, 1878.

d. A bowl, 8in. in diameter, found in Grove Terrace in 1875, and ornamented with game cocks and lions.—*Purchased*, 1875.

II. D. *a.* A fine bowl, 9in. in diameter, showing a pattern and a hunter shooting at a lion. Found at Malton, and *Exhibited by Mrs. Sellers of York*.

b. Another fine bowl, found in York circa 1840, and formerly in the possession of Mr. Wardell of Leeds. It is in. 8¼in diameter, and exhibits an armed soldier and other figures with the maker's name, *Divixti*, on the outside.†—*Mr. John Holmes of Roundhay*, 1881.

* Two embossed bowls from York are in the Bateman Collection, now in the Sheffield Museum.
† Figured in Bowman's Reliquiæ Eboracenses, p.p. 11—12.

c.   One half of a fine bowl, 9in. in diameter, found in York, with the festoon and tassel border, and, below, a scroll of a vine-branch, with birds pecking at the fruit.—*Mr. I. Tuke Holmes,* 1847.

d.   A beautiful bowl, 9½in. in diameter, found on the Mount, and covered with animals and birds, human figures and deities, among whom is Diana with her bow and fawn.— *Purchased, circa* 1840.

III. D.   This compartment contains specimens of the richly embossed and glazed pottery of the first century, which is so rarely met with.   The greater part of it was found in an ancient midden-heap, on the site of the Fine Art Exhibition, and was admirably mended by the late Dr. Gibson.

a.   Part of a bowl with foliage and stags.   Found under the donor's house in Bootham.—*Dr. Gibson,* 1879.

b.   A noble bowl, 9½in. in diameter, ornamented with scrolls and leaves and with a brilliant glaze.   Found under the Exhibition building.   *The Exhibition Committee,* 1878.

c.   Parts of two other bowls of a similar character and from the same place.

d.   A great part of another bowl found in Blossom Street.— *Purchased,* 1876.

e.   A portion of a low, deep bowl ornamented with leaves and borders of great beauty.   Found under the new Entrance Lodge, in 1874.

f.   Another large bowl, from the Exhibition grounds, of beautiful glaze and design, 9in. in diameter.—*The Exhibition Committee,* 1878.

IV. D.   *a.*   Part of a large bowl, 10in. in diameter, with ivy-leaves.   Found near the Mount.—*The Cook Collection,* 1872.

b.   A part of a bowl, ornamented with scrolls of ivy and medallions, with various animals.

c. The greater part of a bowl, 9½in. in diameter, decorated with a string of captives chained together by the neck.— *From the Railway Excavations*, 1873.

d. A bowl, 9in. in diameter, found in East Mount Road, in 1872, and ornamented with figures.—*Rev. J. Raine*, 1872.

V. D. *a.* The greater part of a bowl, found in Grove Terrrace in 1878, covered with a hunting scene, boars, lions, etc.

b. Half of a very fine bowl, with leaves and figures, found in Stonegate in 1879.

c. Portions of a beautiful bowl, on which Diana with her bow and fawn is a prominent feature.—*From the Railway Excavations*, 1873.

d. Part of a bowl with medallions and gladiators.—*Found near Holgate Bridge*, 1876.

e. Part of a bowl, representing love-scenes.—*From Holgate Bridge*, 1876.

f. Part of a bowl covered with a hunting-scene.—*Found in Priory Street*, 1874.

VI. D. A large number of bases of Samian vessels, many of which exhibit parts of the pattern.

VII. D. Portions of Samian bowls.

a. Part of a bowl, found in Bootham, showing incidents in the life of Hercules.—*Dr. Gibson*, 1879.

b. A great part of a bowl, found in East Mount Road in 1872, ornamented with ivy-leaves and figures.—*Rev. J. Raine*, 1872.

c. Part of a bowl with wild animals on it.

d. A large fragment of a finely glazed bowl, covered with leaves and figures. Found near the Mount.—*The Cook Collection*, 1872.

e. Part of a small bowl, with mounted hunters and wild beasts. Found under the City wall, 1874.

f. A part of **a** large bowl, with medallions and figures.—
Railway Excavations, 1878.

g. Part of a large bowl, with a military figure and a single
vine-leaf, alternately.

VIII. D. A series of covered cups or bowls, plain, with a
protecting rim.

IX. D. Jugs, infant's feeding bottles, cups, and salt-
cellars.

X. D. Vessels of graduated sizes, round and fluted, said
to have been for vinegar and other uses, and richly glazed.

XI. D. *a.* A cup, ornamented with ivy-leaves, given by
Dr. Gibson in 1878, and other beautiful examples of the same
decoration.

b. Two cups, and many pieces of Samian ware, with
incised patterns. *

XII. D. Vessels, and many fragments, with the lotus leaf
and flower upon the rim, in very beautiful variety.

XIII. D. Fragments of pottery, embossed with the following subjects, *i.e.,* wolf-hunting, game-cocks, ostriches,
porpoises, sea-horses, etc.

XIV. D. A beautiful collection of pieces, ornamented with
branches and leaves.

XV. and XVI. D. A large collection of scrolls and borders,
arranged so as to show the charming designs used by the
potters, which cannot easily be surpassed.

XVII. D. Parts of lofty, upright bowls or cups, some of
which are most choice.

XVIII. D. Numerous fragments of embossed vessels.

Case E.

This Case contains an example of a peculiar mode of
sepulture in very common use at Eburacum. The body was

* *cf.* Mr. C. R. Smith's London, p. 93.

laid in a coffin in which liquified gypsum had been poured, and was then covered with it to a certain height. This practice was probably desirable for sanitary purposes. The material also, as it hardened, retained an impression of the body. The remains in this Case are those of a female and a child ; the body of the latter having been placed, as the impression in the plaster represents it, between the legs of the former, who was most probably its mother. The garments in which they were buried appeared to have been ornamented with crimson or purple stripes,* of a texture of something like velvet or plush ; portions of the coloured fibre being found adhering to the lime. The stone coffin containing these remains was discovered in July, 1851, about three feet below the surface, near Skeldergate Postern, by the side of the road leading to Bishopthorpe. It is deposited in the ruins of St. Leonard's Hospital (marked II), with the tomb mentioned in the next article.

The lead coffin below this stand contained the body of a child, and was found in 1872, in the road leading from the City to the new Coal Depôts.

Case F.

I. F.   In this Case there is a continuation of the Collection of Samian ware. We have in the first compartment Cupids and Deities.

II. F.   Hunting scenes.   The ibex ; deer ; wild-boar ; bear.

III. F.   Fragments of vessels, which very rarely occur. Among them are pieces of pottery turned on the wheel with incised patterns ; specimens with white slip † ; examples of

* Isidore Hisp. xi. i. 123. Purpuræ vestes mortuis præbentur.
† cf. Lee's Isca Silurum, ed. 1862, plate xlvii.

handles of vessels; and pieces with raised figures. Among the latter are

a. A figure, remarkable for its high relief and superior execution. It is supposed to represent Atys, the Phrygian shepherd and priest of Cybele, with his staff in one hand, and a castanet in the other, and, instead of being stamped on the vessel, has been separately moulded, and then carefully affixed by a graving tool. Specimens of this mode of ornamentation are very rare.†

b. A portion of the rim of a mortar decorated with figures in high relief. A figure of a river-god, or Silenus, is laid asleep, with the mouth or vent of the mortar under his left arm. Before him is a bird settling on a basket of fruit, which a Cupid is trying to capture. Found in Blossom Street.— *Mr. E. Swaine*, 1874.

c. A portion of a red deer in high relief. Found in the Railway Excavations, 1873.

d. Fragments of two other vessels, one found at Clifton, the other near the new Railway Station.

IV. F. Hunting the lion; and lioness; combats with the *urus* or wild-bull.

V. F. Chariot-races; gladiators; hares and rabbits.

VI. F. Parts of vessels selected to shew their size and thickness.

VII. and VIII. F. Parts of large *paterœ* and dishes.

IX. F. A perfect mortar (*mortarium*), used for culinary purposes. The surface of the interior is thickly studded with particles of silicious stone or quartz, to aid the process of trituration. The rim is furnished with an ornamental opening through which mixtures in a liquid state were poured. The opening was in the shape of the head of a lion or bat, of

† See Mr. C. R. Smith, Journal of the Archæological Association, vol. iv. p. 11, and the Catalogue of his Museum of London Antiquities, p. 30.

which this compartment presents numerous examples. Other portions of mortars more or less complete.

X. F. A large fragment of a moulded bowl, with other examples. *Pateræ*. One from Lincoln, presented by Mrs. Hutton, 1848.

XI. F. Bowls and *pateræ*, several very fine and perfect.

XII. F. Very numerous fragments of dishes and *pateræ*.

XIII. and XIV. F. Specimens of black ware cast in Samian moulds. Many fragments with letters and other marks roughly scatched upon them, generally called *Graffiti*.

XV. F. A large collection of potters' marks. Some of a peculiar kind in the form of ornaments, etc. Others occurring on the outsides of the vessels among the foliage and figures. On several there is a double name, as if the master and fore-man of the pottery had distinct marks.

In the drawers of Case K is preserved a collection of the marks of between 400 and 500 potters, all found in York and stamped across the bottoms of Samian vessels. The kilns in which many of these vessels were made are being discovered abroad, with some of the original stamps and moulds used by the potters. We are thus enabled to discover whence the Romans derived much of the pottery which was in use in Britain. It came from the great manufactories in France and Germany.

XVI. F. A large variety of pieces of base Samian ware, probably manufactured in England in imitation of the genuine pottery. The difference in execution and glaze is very observ-able. On a *patera* the maker has forged the name of a well-known potter, Severianus. A piece of Severianus' handiwork is placed beside the forgery to shew the contrast.

XVII. F. Specimens of the mode of rivetting pieces of fractured Samian vessels with lead. Examples of the mending of ordinary vessels with the same material.

XVIII. F. *a.* A cast from a pig of lead, found with another on Hayshaw Moor, near Pateley Bridge, in 1734, and bequeathed by Sir Wm. Ingilby, Bart., to the British Museum, to which it came in 1772. It bears the following inscription :

IMP·CAES·DOMITIANO·AVG·COS·VII.

denoting that the original was cast in the seventh consulship of the Emperor Domitian ; *i.e.* A.D. 80 or 81. Another, found at the same time, is preserved in the muniment room at Ripley castle.*—The Archæological Institute,* 1846.

b. A leaden mortar found in Park Street ; a spoon of lead, and other objects of the same metal. Several crucibles.

Case G.

This case contains the remains and the impression of the body which had been deposited in the large tomb (marked I.) placed in the room under the chapel of the infirmary of St. Leonard's Hospital (see p. 14). The body appears to have been placed in a coffin of wood, which was then filled with gypsum. The coffin had perished, so that upon opening the tomb nothing appeared but the hardened gypsum, containing the skull and a few bones, and a distinct impression of the body. Minute portions of coffin, supposed to be cedar, are imbedded in the gypsum ; and a few small fragments were found in the tomb, in one of which is enclosed an iron nail.

Below this case is a small coffin of lead for a child, discovered during the excavations for the first Railway Station.

I. H. Three bowls, and other specimens of light brown ware, with minute patterns impressed upon them.

II. H. Fragments of so-called Durobrivian ware, consisting of a beautiful variety of dogs, and other animals. Also, many specimens of scroll-work.

* *cf.* Hübner's Inscrr. Brit., 223.

III. H. Pieces of bright, black, glazed ware, several of which have letters upon them. A beautiful variety.

IV. H. Examples of patterns turned upon the wheel; white colours upon red; red-painting upon straw-colour. Parts of a noble vessel with handles, and heads and fir-cones alternately. Part of a cup with a double border, with circles and stars. A fragment of a vessel with pink lines over a dark ground.

V. H. Numerous examples of red colouring upon white ware. Necks of jugs ornamented with female heads.* Heads of cocks.

VI. H. Specimens of pottery over which sand seems to have been sprinkled when it was soft.

VII. H. A series of urns and bowls of red ware. One is fluted like the pottery in XIV. B.

VIII. H. A large number of small vessels of red and white ware of a peculiar shape. Several lids of vessels.

IX. H. Vessels with a frill around the edge. One is of white ware with a double frill. Possibly they were flower vases.†

X. H. Some elegant vessels of light brown ware, which have been turned on a wheel. The large lid behind them was found near the Yorkshire Bank.

XI. H. A number of shallow, round bowls. Two have been painted. That in the centre (from the Cook Collection) is coloured to resemble wood.

XII. H. Three vessels in the shape of a human head. One was found in Blossom Street, presented by Mr E. Swaine. *b*. From Priory Street, 1874. *c*. A small specimen, from Fishergate, presented by Mr. Ralph Weatherley, 1855. There are fragments of some twenty other vessels of a like kind.

---

* *cf.* Mr. C. R. Smith's Catalogue of his Museum, p. 19; and his London, p. 86.
† *cf.* Journal. Arch. Assocn., xiv., 337; C. R. Smith's London, 83.

F

XIII. H.   Necks of *Ampullæ*, or jugs, many of them of choice and rare kinds.

XIV.—XVIII. H.   A large collection of culinary vessels in grey and black ware, consisting of pots, colanders, mortars, and dishes of various kinds.

Case I.

This Case contains the impression of the body of a female. The texture of the garment in which the body was clothed may be clearly perceived in the impression.   The feet, which had been crossed, had sandals on them, as is evident from the marks of the nails of the soles.   The nails themselves, No. 1, were found in the coffin.   A very small portion of the bones remained ;   but all the teeth, No. 2, excepting one, were found with the enamel undecayed.   Just above the left shoulder, a small portion of a gold ring appeared ; and the plaster surrounding it being carefully removed, various ornaments were brought to light, consisting of fragments of large jet rings ; two ear-rings of fine gold ; two bracelets ; several bronze rings, Nos. 3, 4 ; three finger-rings, No. 5 ; and two necklaces, No. 6.   One of the necklaces is formed of glass, yellow and green ; the other of small beads of coral and blue glass. The beads in both instances had been strung on very fine twisted silver wire, which had almost entirely perished.   A fragment is preserved in No. 7.   The rude coffin which contained the body was found in Heslington Field.   It is placed in the Multangular tower, and marked H. F.—*Mr. N. E. Yarburgh*, 1831.

In the same Case is the cast of another body, found in the garden of the new Station Hotel in 1877.

Against the wall is hung a cast of a portion of a skeleton, ound in 1828, in a stone coffin at Arentsburgh* in Holland.

It represents a Roman, disposed for burial, with fibula and bracelets, and illustrates the system of interment which prevailed at Eburacum.—*The Society of Antiquaries, London,* 1875.

CASE J.

In the centre is the impression of the body of an infant in gypsum, found in a small stone coffin during the Railway Excavations in 1876.

In the same case are the following curiosities :

a. Portions of statuettes of Venus in white clay, found on the Mount and in the Railway Excavations. These figures are found in great numbers in France.*

b. One half of a finely polished tablet of green-stone or slate, which seems to have been set in a frame.† The name CANDIDUS is scratched upon it. Discovered in 1868 near the Scarbro' Railway bridge.—*Rev. Wm. Greenwell,* 1872.

c. Fragments of pottery. One inscribed QVRIO,—from Mr. F. Calvert. Another, MERC,—from the Railway Excavations. Two Samian fragments, with names on them, which seem to be in Greek characters,‡—both from York.

d. About one third of a mould for making a Samian bowl, in fine preservation, and the only specimen as yet found in Britain.—*Railway Excavations,* 1874.

e. The greater part of an alabaster vase, used by the Romans for embalming. Found in Priory Street in 1874.

Roman coin moulds, found at Lingwell-gate, near Wakefield. Such moulds have been discovered in other parts of England, near ancient Roman roads and stations. Mr. Artis found a great number of them, with the apparatus for casting coins, in

* See Mr. C. R. Smith's London, 109—10; and his Collectanea, vi. 58, etc.
† A similar object has been found at Wroxeter, *cf* Journal Arch. Assocn., xv., 326.
‡ See a paper by Mr. C. R. Smith, in Journal of Arch. Assocn., iv. 19—20, with an engraving ; also his London, p. 108.

the extensive potteries of Durobrivæ, in Northamptonshire. In France also, especially near Lyons, they have been met with in great abundance. They are formed of clay, hardened by fire to the consistency of brick. Each tablet, with the exception of those intended to be placed at the ends of the pile in the process of casting, has two impressions of a minted coin, taken when the clay was moist, the obverse being on one side, the reverse on the other; but the tablets placed at the ends of the pile have only one impression. A small notch is cut on the edge of each tablet, by which, when the piles were made, and arranged either two or three together, the melted metal passed into the mould. It has been supposed that these moulds "were used by the Roman armies for the purpose of paying the soldiers when they were at a distance from home, and when there was a deficiency in the military chest." But another opinion is, that they were tools of counterfeiters of the lawful currency. All the moulds discovered bear the heads of Sept. Severus and his successors, down to Posthumus.* The obverses of the moulds here exhibited are all those of the family of Severus.—*Rev. W. V. Harcourt, 1823; Mrs. Davies, 1825; Mr. Pett of Huddersfield, 1846.*

f. Seven lead seals found at Brough in Westmerland, six of which were given by the Rev. Dr. Simpson of Kirkby Stephen, in 1880. Very large quantities of them have been found there. They are stamped on both sides with letters, and are supposed to have been given to recruits.

g. A large cinerary urn, found in front of the New Station Hotel in 1878. The ashes are preserved, with a stone with which the urn was covered.

h. Another cinerary urn, exhibited as it was found on the Mount in 1877. It is laid, in a reversed position, on a flat

* See Numism. Journal, ii., p. 567; Numism, Chron., i., p. 47, et seq. Archæo-logia, xxiv., 349; Bowman's Reliquiæ Ebor., 41—4; Thoresby's Catalogue of his Museum, ed. Whitaker, 107—8.

stone, and surrounded, for protection, by three others. The mouth of the urn was hermetically sealed up with lead, which is still preserved.

i. Several Roman urns, and other curiosities, from the -Museum at Kertch* in the Crimea, given by the Rev. J. J. Harrison, in 1856. An amphora from the same place is on the top of Case B.

j. Two Roman jugs and a lamp from Kolea in Algeria, given by Mrs. Norcliffe in 1869.

Under this Case are placed a number of querns for grinding corn, several of which are probably of the Roman era.

CASE K.

This is a large Case constructed in 1872-3, to hold the specimens of Roman Metal Work, Implements, and Ornaments of Bone, Jet, &c.

I. K. *a.* i. A cock in bronze, found in the Multangular Tower. This was the badge of the Fourth Cohort of Gauls, which was stationed at Little Chesters on the Roman Wall.† ii. An eagle within a double circle in which has been an inscription in excised letters, of which one letter only remains. It seems to have been similar to one found at High Rochester in Northumberland.‡ iii. An ostrich, from the Cook Collection. iv. A peacock, from the R. E., 1875, and other birds.

b. i. A bovine head in bronze, found at Aldborough‖ in 1794. A similar relic has been found, with Roman remains, at North Waltham, Hants.—*Dr. Murray, of Scarbro',* 1828. ii. A toad in bronze.§

---

* *cf.* Journal Arch. Assocn. vi., 259 ; xiii., 299, etc.
† *cf.* Lapidarium Septentrionale, 248, 270, 649.
‡ *cf.* Ibid., p. 303.
‖ Engraved in Ecroyd Smith's Isurium, pl. xxv. *a.*
§ Altars with toads carved upon them have been found at Chesters & Lanchester. *cf.* Lapid. Septent. Nos. 115, 693-6.

c. A small tablet of bronze, 3in. long by 2in. broad, originally coated with silver, to the back of which another of the same form, but of a smaller size, is adhering : found in the Excavation for the Old Railway Station, circa 1840. On each plate is a Greek inscription in punctured uncial letters :

i.
        ΘΕΟΙϹ
        ΤΟΙϹ ΤΟΥ ΠΓΕ
        ΜΟΝΙΚΟΥ ΠΡΑΙ
        ΤΩΡΙΟΥ ϹΚΡΙΒ.
        ΛΗ(Μ)ΗΤΡΙΟϹ

ii.
        ΩΚΕΑΝΩΙ
        ΚΑΙ ΤΗΘΥΙ
        ΔΗΜΗΤΡΙ. .

That is,

i. Θεοῖς τοῖς τοῦ ἡγεμονικοῦ πραιτωρίου Σκιβ. Δημήτριος.
ii. Ωκεανῶ κὰι Τηθύι Δημήτριος.

The tablets are votive offerings appended to shrines by a person called Scribonius Demetrius. The first is dedicated to the Gods of the General's Prætorium which contained altars to the heathen deities ;* the second, to Oceanus and Tethys, marine divinities whom a voyager would be anxious to propitiate. A valuable paper on these inscriptions by the Rev. S. S. Lewis, of Cambridge, appears in the Transactions of the Society.—*The Directors of the North Eastern Railway.*

d. A small gold earring, out of which the stone has dropped. Found in a stone coffin on the Mount.—*The Cook Collection,* 1872.

* This, as Mr. Kenrick remarked, explains the unwillingness of the Jews to enter into Pilate's Prætorium, especially at Passover-tide, lest they should be defiled by the heathen deities who were represented there. These tablets have been engraved and serve as an illustration to Farrar's Life of Christ, under S. John xviii. 28. *cf.* Transactions of Y. P. S., 1876, pp. 106-110.

e. A thin plate of pure gold, measuring about 1in. by ¾in., bearing an inscription in two lines, rudely and slightly formed. To what system of writing the characters in the upper line belong, or what is their meaning, is altogether uncertain ; but the lower line being in Greek characters, is sufficiently legible : ΦΝΕΒΕΝΝΟΥΘ. Though expressed in Greek characters, the word is probably Coptic ; and the interpretation of it, " Lord of the Gods ; " but to whom this title was meant to be applied it is not easy to decide.* It was found in the excavations for the Old Railway Station, and was probably an amulet or spell, belonging to a disciple of one of the Egyptian sects of Gnostics which prevailed during the second and third centuries of the Christian era. This relic of ancient superstition may have been brought to York from Egypt in the reign of Septimius Severus, who was much devoted to Egyptian superstition.†— *Mr. Thomas Allis*, 1848.

f. On a small stand, a series of finger-rings of various metals, and engraved stones. Among which are : i. A large, hollow gold ring, found near the White House, in 1880, and set with a carnelian, bearing a bird.—*Purchased.* ii. Another gold ring, found on the Mount, set with a Niccolo, on which a stork is engraved, which was adopted by the gens Cæcilia as a symbol of piety.—*Bequeathed by Miss Widdowson*, 1877. iii. A small hexagonal gold ring,‡ found whilst making the Old Railway Station.—*Mr. Thos. Allis*, 1848. iv. A ring of

* See Proceedings of the Yorkshire Philosophical Society, vol. i., p. 100.
† Spartian, c. 17.
‡ A ring, similar to this, has been found in Northumberland. *cf.* Lapidarium Septentr., and at Barton in Oxfordshire. *cf.* Arch. Journal, vi. 290.

A gold ring, set with an intaglio on ribbon onyx, and found in a stone coffin at York, is in the Museum at Audley End. *cf.* Journal Arch. Inst. vii. 195.

A Roman gold ring, found in Tanner Row, was exhibited in 1846, by Rev. D. R. Currer, at the meeting of the Arch. Inst. at York.

Two other Roman gold rings, found recently in the City, are now in the hands of a private collector; one, set with a fine ruby, was taken from the finger of Flavius gold, wreathed and twisted at the end, found under the City Wall near the Old Railway Station.—*Rev. C. Wellbeloved.* v. A piece of ornamental work in gold, with a bead of green glass, probably part of a bracelet, or ear-ring. vi. A large silver ring, found in 1875 on Barker Hill, and inscribed *Deo Sucelo*, a Deity hitherto unknown.—*Purchased.* vii. Another ring of silver, from the New Railway Excavations, found in 1875, and inscribed TOT. viii. A carnelian, with a Victory on it driving a *biga*, found in Church Street in 1878. *Purchased.* ix. The rape of Cassandra, on a similar stone, found in a garden in Blossom Street in 1878.—*Mr. A. Valentine.* x. An onyx bearing a marriage type, *i.e.* two doves, a cornucopiæ, two wheat ears, and a poppy head.—*Bought of Mr. J. Browne's Exors.*, 1877. xi. Jupiter Serapis in blue paste, helmeted and throned, with a lance in left hand and an eagle in his right, from the Railway excavations of 1873.—*The Directors of the N.E. Railway.*

g. A thin plate of gold, about 2in. long by 1½in. broad, with a small hole at each end, found close to a skull in the Roman cemetery. A similar plate was discovered a few years since in a marble tomb at Athens, which had been fixed in a head-dress as an ornament. In the mouth of the lady, to whom our gold plate belonged, was a denarius of Severus, FORTUNA AUG.—*The Directors of the N.E. Railway,* 1872.

h. On a large stand, a very fine collection of *fibulæ* and specimens of enamelling.

i. A great number of *fibulæ*. The most frequent use of the *fibula* was to fasten together parts of the loose dress called the *amictus*, or shawl, over the right shoulder. Among

Bellator, the Decurion; the other, which is curiously ornamented, has an onyx with a kneeling archer, bending his bow.

A magnificent cameo, representing the head of a youthful fawn, of the finest period of art, was found in 1828, in the garden of Mr. R. Davies, in St. Leonard's Place, and is now in the possession of his nephew, Rev. A. S. Porter.

these there are as many as eight of silver, one of which has been finely enamelled. Two are in the shape of serpents.

ii. A large collection of enamelled ornaments, some of great beauty in colour and design, consisting of fibulæ, scent boxes, studs, clasps, &c. One fibula is in the shape of a horse, another of a cock, others of dolphins, and an eagle. Among them is the finest boutton that has been discovered in England. It was found in front of the Station Hotel * in 1878.

i. An ear-drop of garnet, found under the City Wall in 1874. Part of an amber ring, from Malton. An ear-ring of amber, exhibited by Mr. E. Bean. Two amber beads. Three small jet bracelets, from the Railway Excavations, 1875.

j. A series of jet ornaments, unexampled in number and beauty. The Romans soon utilized the jet which they would find at Whitby. All of these ornaments are from York, and have been chiefly discovered during the Railway Excavations.

i. A series of bangles, or armlets of jet or Kimmeridge coal,—one of large size, 4in. in diameter. It has been suggested that these may have formed part of the head-gear.

ii. Two armlets found on the arms of a skeleton, on the Mount, in 1824.—*The Hargrove Collection*, 1847.

iii. A beautifully carved head of Medusa in jet, which may have been worn as a *bulla* or drop to a necklace, or a magical amulet.† Found in York.—*Mr. M. Carr*, 1841.

iv. A *bulla* or drop, pierced for a string, with two heads on it, a man and a woman. Another, smaller, with a man's head. A third, found in the Railway Excavations in 1874, representing a large, coiled snake. A fourth, of coarse material, with heads of man, woman, and child.

* *cf.* Isca Silurum, ed. 1862, p. 28; see also Cat. of Museum of Arch. Inst. at York, in 1846; several of these ornaments are engraved in Wellbeloved's Eburacum.

† *cf.* Collect. Antiqua, i., 174.

F 2

v. A large plain bangle, with a beautiful polish, from the Railway Excavations, 1876. A workman brought it out of the ground on the point of his pick-axe.

vi. A bracelet, composed of many pieces put together, 4in. in diameter, of great beauty and fine workmanship. Found on the Mount.

vii. Another bracelet from the Mount, worked in grooves. *Miss Atkinson.*

viii. A number of miscellaneous fragments, a scarabæus, beads, etc., etc.

ix. A set of twelve beads, a beautifully cut bangle (from the Hargrove Collection), and a seal-ring with a curious Eastern device upon it. All these were found together in a stone coffin, in 1840. With them were found the extraordinary number of fourteen jet pins with plain round heads, and two broken implements of bone, which had probably been used for netting.

x. Finger rings and a fibula.

xi. A very fine series of pins, more than thirty in number, some of them with beautifully carved heads.

k. i. Three jet hair pins found in the R. E. 1874, in a stone coffin under the head of a lady. One is more than 7in. long and has run through the back hair. It is perforated at the lower end, and a piece of wood or metal must have been inserted, fastened on to a nut or roundlet of jet (which lies by the pins) to prevent the pin from slipping. ii. The greater part of a similar pin, 5½in. long, of a cable pattern, used, no doubt, for the same purpose.—*Mr. F. Nelson,* 1877.

l. i. Two fine hair pins of jet, from a lady's grave.—*Railway Excavations,* 1877. ii. Four jet bracelets with beads, &c., from another grave.—*Railway Excavations,* 1876. iii. Four pins of jet and two of bone, taken from below the feet of a corpse in a stone coffin. One of the pins is cut for the admission of a stone on each face.—*Railway Excavations,* 1876.

m. A very finely cut bangle, a fine finger ring, parts of chain necklace, all of jet, and a grand pin and needle of ivory, 9 and 6½ inch long. All from one grave.—*Railway Excavations,* 1874.

n. A suite of ornaments taken from a stone coffin found at the corner of the garden of the New Station Hotel, in which a lady was interred, consisting of a small glass bottle, placed at the top of the coffin, above the head; two bangles from below the feet of the corpse, one on either side; parts of another bangle, carved, and of some bone armlets from the right wrist. These bone armlets were not cut out of one solid piece, but out of several, which were united by bindings of lead or copper.—*Railway Excavations,* 1874.

o. Fragments of pins, bangles, and other ornaments of jet and Kimmeridge coal.

p. Three pieces of Kimmeridge coal from which rings or bangles have been cast, and bearing the holes by which they have been fixed to the lathe. This coal, or very coarse jet, takes its name from a place called Kimmeridge on the coast of Dorsetshire, where it has been worked in very large quantities.[*]—*Dr. Smart, of Northiam,* 1859.

q. Several blocks of jet in the rough, and some pieces partially prepared for pins, found in the Railway excavations, 1873, &c. Jet was highly esteemed by the ancients on account of the medicinal and supernatural powers it was supposed to possess.[†]

---

[*] *cf.* Journal Arch. Ass., I. 325.

[†] Other ornaments in jet, &c., were found during the two Railway Excavations, which although they were assigned with the other products of the diggings to the Museum have been withheld, in some instances by persons who ought to have known better. Among these objects the Curator may mention a necklace of large beads with a central drop in the form of a rose.

II. K. A large and very fine series of implements and ornaments in bone and ivory, found in York.

a, *b*, *c*. Three stands of combs of various shapes ; one of them was found adhering to the head of a lady with a large hair-pin.

d. A tablet of bone, 2¼in. long by ¾in. broad, with the following incised inscription :

DOMINE VICTOR
VINCAS FELIX.

It was found in the Railway excavations in 1878, at the breast of a skeleton, and probably belonged to a gladiator. The letters are probably of the third or fourth century.*

e. Two remarkable instruments of ivory, 12in. long, shaped like half a boat with a long spike or handle at the end. They were found in a stone coffin during the Railway excavations, in 1874, on the left side of a Roman lady, and were perhaps the handles of fans. The cavity may have held the quills of the feathers of peacocks or some other bird, and have been padded or quilted over

f. A portion of what seems to have been a circus ticket, with an inscription. It has been split and little more than a third-of it remains.

g. A large stand covered with implements in bone and ivory, consisting of needles and skewers ; counters or buttons; instruments for netting or knitting; implements used by potters; and many other objects which it is impossible to describe. Those marked C. are from the Cook Collection which was bought and presented to the Museum in 1872, by the Rev. J. Kenrick, Curator of Antiquities.

h. A collection of large hair-pins on a stand, with ornamented ends. Two of them terminate with a cross.

* Felix potest gladiator fuisse, cui tessera victoriam auguratur in Victoris nomine ludens. Domini appellatio eo tempore communis jam facta erat.— (Hübner. Inscriptiones Britanniæ Christianæ, 85.)

i. On another stand is a small collection of choice pins and needles exhibited by Mr. E. Bean. On the same stand is a very curious instrument, of which examples have been found among British as well as Roman remains. It is perforated horizontally as well as diagonally, and when cleaning it several little pins or wedges of bone were discovered inside. Its use is as yet conjectural. Another example is on stand marked *n.*

j. On the floor of the Case are several miscellaneous objects. A boar's tusk which (with another) has made a torque for the neck ;* parts of bangles of ivory ; handles of bone for whips ; and lengths of ivory fastened together with lead, and resembling the frame or bands of a modern parasol.

k. i. Several curious spoons ; the bowl of one is dyed dark green. ii. Several spoon-shaped *fibulæ* by which the two sides of the *toga* have been fastened together in front.

l. A small collection of pins and needles from Colchester, for comparison. One of them has a gold head.—*Mr. W. Whincupp,* 1847.

m. A large stand covered with some hundreds of pins of bone and ivory, of every shape and variety. Among them is one with a silver head, and three with heads of agate.

n. A stand covered with handles of knives, one retaining the blade. One in the shape of a sphinx is beautifully carved.

o. On a stand, the pommel of a sword ; several spindle-whorls, and an ornamented counter.†

p. One half of a hollowed instrument of ivory for shaping pins. The pin near it fits the groove, and was found with it. —*Railway Excavations,* 1873. On the same stand is a large hair-pin only partially wrought.

q. Deers' horn cut into lengths for the use of the maker of pins ; and a pin found with them. We are thus able to

* C. R. Smith's Richborough, p. 110.
† *cf.* Lee's Isca Silurum, p. 30; Catalogue of the Edinburgh Museum.

illustrate the manufacture of these objects.—*Railway Excav-ations*, 1873.

III. K.   This side of the Case is occupied chiefly by objects in bronze.

a.   A bronze bas-relief, of fine workmanship, representing Victory rewarding a conqueror.   It is said, on the back, to have been found at Aldborough (Isurium), but it is more probably of Cinque-Cento work.   From the collection of John Croft, F.S.A.—*Rev. R. Croft,* 1824.

b.   Several curious objects of bronze discovered in the Roman Cemetery in 1872, by the side of a skeleton.   They consist of a small bust of a deity ; a beautifully modelled vase which contained several coriander seeds ; a rough piece of copper, and fragments of handles.   Chains were also dis-covered, but they fell into pieces.   It is conjectured that these remarkable objects were votive offering for a child.

c.   A pair of compasses, the branches of which have been broken ; remarkable for the construction of the joint.

Also a *regula*, or foot-rule of bronze.   The graduations have almost entirely disappeared ; but when extended it corresponds with the Roman foot 11.604 inches.   The stay at the back, turning upon a pivot, is imperfect, but the studs on the opposite limb, which it was designed to receive in corres-ponding notches, for the purpose of keeping the rule straight when fully opened, still remain.   A similar instrument has been discovered at Caerleon.*

With these are two or three fragments of other rules, discovered in the excavations of 1872, with the graduations marked upon them.   One of them bears the Christian monogram.†

---

* Isca Silurum, by J. E. Lee, p. 69. Arch. Journal, viiL, 160.

† *cf.* Hübner's Inscr. Brit. Christianæ, p. 80.

d. A statuette of a female having a *patera* (or perhaps a cymbal) in her right hand ; found near the Multangular Tower. —*Mr. G. Thorp.* A small bronze figure of Hercules with his club on his shoulder.—*The Cook Collection.* A statuette óf Cupid, holding a bird in one hand, and apparently a bunch of grapes in the other. A small head found under the City wall at the entrance to the Old Railway Station. A small foot of bronze.

e. Scale-beams, entire or fragmentary. The arms of one of them have been formed to move on joints near the axis. On the same stand is a weight belonging to a *statera*, or Roman steel-yard, representing a head covered with a cap or casque. Other weights.

f. On a stand. A large collection of bronze articles found on Fremington Hagg, near Reeth, in Swaledale. They have probably formed the stock-in-trade of some travelling artizan. They consist of horse-harness, plated with silver, and ornamented with engraved patterns. The other articles on the stand, of which there is a great variety, are such as are usually found in Roman Stations.—*Captain Harland.*

g. A number of Roman locks, found in 1874-5 ; also an iron key found in 1867 in a lead coffin, on the breast of a young man.

h. Several pieces of bronze from the recent Railway excavations, of doubtful use.

i. The point of a scabbard of a sword ; a vessel for filling lamps with oil ; and several other things.

j. Several handles in bronze, one terminating in the head of a swan.

k. A large stand covered with objects of a most miscellaneous character, such as bosses, keys, ring-keys, &c., &c. A ring-key served the purpose, not only of a key, but also of a signet ring, an impression of the wards being made on the wax, placed on the mouth of vessels containing household stores to secure them from being pillaged by slaves.

l. Two boxes of lead and bronze; a lead nail; a small square of pot, found in a lead coffin, in 1873.

m. A foot and two legs in bronze and iron. They are probably votive offerings, a custom adopted afterwards by the Christian church. One leg was discovered near Micklegate Bar, in 1868; the other in the Railway excavations, 1872.

n. *Cochlearia,* or spoons, having one end pointed for the purpose of taking snails (*cochleæ*) out of their shells and eating them. With the other end, which is generally broad and hollow, eggs, &c., were eaten. The large snail, now called *Helix Pomatia,* is yet used as food in several parts of Europe. It was reckoned a great delicacy by the ancient Romans,* and was fattened by them for the table. A snail-shell, from the recent Railway excavations, is laid near the spoons.

o. A number of *ligulæ,* or smaller spoons, with long stems, supposed to have been used " for taking ointment and prepared oils from long-necked bottles."† It is possible that some of the spoons on this stand may have been used for surgical purposes.

IV. K. *a.* Several bells upon a stand; one is of silver, and another retains its clapper.

b. Parts of a glass bottle; bone and bronze armlets and chains; a coin of Crispus; and a fragment of ornamented bone with a shell attached to it.—*Railway Excavations,* 1874.

c. A small chain-bracelet from Colchester.

d. On a large stand, a collection of bronze ornaments.

---

* See Da Costa's Brit. Conchol. p. 67. The pointed end may have served another purpose. The Romans were accustomed, when they had eaten an egg, a snail, or a shell-fish, to pierce or break the shell.—PLIN., N. H., xxviii., 4.

† C. R. Smith's Richborough, p. 103.

i. Pins. Two are of silver, and two have glass heads. ii. Keepers or holdfasts. iii. Cocks of vessels. iv. The handle of a knife in bronze, representing a leopard issuing from foliage, spotted with inlaid studs of silver.* v. Part of a silver mirror, and several ear-rings. vi. *Styli* or gravers. The *stylus* was an instrument used for writing upon waxed tablets; one end being pointed for marking the letters; the other, flat for the purpose of making the wax smooth, and of effacing what has been written. vii. Bronze needles and bodkins of various kinds.

e. On a stand. A pair of bracelets from the arm-bones of a skeleton. Two other pairs from the Railway excavations, 1874, 1876.

f. A silver necklet. From the Railway excavations, 1874.

g. Fragments of bronze chains. A chain of beads, that in the centre taking the form of a shell of a crab.

h. A number of what are believed to be surgical instruments. They consist of a pair of nippers with a sliding ring, called *tenaculum*; a knife, resembling the modern scalpel. The others are probes, &c.

i. A beautiful and perfect chain of bronze, with a smaller one of beads of amber and blue glass. With these were found a number of fragments of ivory bracelets, &c.—*Railway Excavations*, 1874.

j. On a large stand. A great number of bronze armlets, of various patterns and sizes.

k. Four bronze armlets, prettily engraved, found in the Roman Cemetery in 1872.

l. A pair of fine bracelets, found on the Mount in 1874.

m. Another pair, one being of jet.—*Railway Excavations*, 1874.

n. A chain of bronze, beads, bracelets, &c., belonging to a child. All found together in the Railway excavations, 1875.

* *cf.* Isca Silurum, ed. 1862, p. 33.

o. The contents of a small box buried with a child, found on the Mount in 1874, consisting of chains, ear-rings, bracelets, &c., of bronze and jet.

p. q. Two pairs of children's bracelets, one of them with a coin of Constantine.—*Railway Excavations*, 1874.

r. A large number of bronze rings of various sizes. It is not known to what purpose they were applied, but they were certainly not worn on the fingers.

Below, in the drawers of this Case, is—i. a miscellaneous collection of Roman ornaments and implements of iron for domestic and military use. ii. A number of fragments of deers' horn, tusks of boars, &c. iii. A number of heads and bones of animals of the Roman era, are preserved in the Museum, with many other objects illustrating the domestic life of that period.

Case L.

In this Case is a model of the remains of the Roman baths which were discovered in excavating for the Old Railway Station, executed by Mr. Baines, sometime sub-curator of the Museum. There are also specimens of the flooring of the baths ; two of them composed of lime and shreds of tiles ; the third of red sand stone. A leaden pipe belonging to the baths* is placed in the lower room of the Hospitium.— *Presented by Mr. Baines*, in 1841.

In this Case are several inscribed and sculptured stones, which, although described among the contents of the lower room, are deposited here for security. They consist of three portions of figures (Nos. 9, 20, 76), a tablet representing a sacrifice to the Local Genius (No. 7) ; and some fragments of an inscription found in the garden of the New Station Hotel, (No. 61.)

* For a long account of these Baths see Wellbeloved's Eburacum.

The Case holds besides : Four tablets, lately in the Campana Collection, from a catacomb in Rome, thus inscribed :

i.   FVRIA . A . Ɔ . L · ·
                      THAIS.

. ii.   OEHKOΛΩI
                     MOΔECTOC

iii.   CALPVRNIA · I. Ɔ. L. HILA.
                 VIX. AN. XXXII.
      VA. PETRONIVS. AL. ALEXANDER
      ANATIARIVS. SIBI. ET. CONIVGI
   SVAE. FECIT. CVM. QVA. CONCORDITER VIXIT.

iv.   MATVTINVS
             ITALIAE
       CONTVBERNALI SVAE.

These stones, small in size, and neatly cut, are very common at Rome, and show the character of funereal inscriptions in a catacomb. They were fixed in a frame underneath an orifice which contained the bones, or the ashes of the deceased.—*Purchased*, 1881.

The Case also contains the following pieces of sculpture in white marble.

a. A head supposed to be that of Bacchus.—*H. Y. Whytehead, M.D., of Easingwold*, 1838.

b. A fine head of some unknown person.—*Mr. C. Rawson*, 1833.

c. A fragment of a hand and part of a bow. Found at Rome.*—*From the Croft Collection*, 1824.

At one end of the Case is a stand or rack, holding six *cadi*, or stone bottles, with portions of two *amphoræ*.

At the other end is a most interesting object, in a glass case specially made for it—the back hair of a Roman lady, taken out of a lead coffin, enclosed in one of stone. (See p. 59.) The hair, which still retains its beautiful auburn

* Under this Case, upon the floor, are several Roman querns.

colour and shape, has two fine jet pins in it, in their original position.

By the side of the hair are some sections of a cast of gypsum, taken out of a stone coffin, showing portions of the cloth* and fine linen in which the corpse was dressed. (See p. 59.)

Case M.

Some playthings of Roman children :—

a. A photograph of the contents of a child's grave found at Cologne, and now in the Mayer Collection at Liverpool, showing its doll, and little pots and pans, &c., for messing and cooking.—*Mr. John Holmes, of Roundhay.*

b. A child's whistle.—*Exhibited by Mr. E. Bean.* *c.* The core of a ball, found in Bootham.—*Dr. Gibson,* 1872.

d. A die of jet, unevenly cut, so that it would only be used by a child. Found in Market Street, 1873.

e. The base of a Samian vessel which a child has used as a paint pot. It still has in it some *minium,* or red paint.—*Railway Excavations,* 1873.

f. Bases of glass and Samian vessels rounded off by children, to play with at a game rasembling our hop-scotch. Their colour enabled them to be easily seen in the grass. They are found in great numbers, and we are indebted to these children for preserving so many potters' marks.

g. Several shells brought to Eburacum from the sea-side by Roman children.

h. Some fragments of an egg-shell, preserved in the bottom of a small vessel.

---

* In the National Museum at Edinburgh, is a piece of cloth, presented by Dr. Hibbert Ware, and taken out of a stone coffin found near Micklegate Bar, in 1838. Mr. Anderson, the curator, thus describes the cloth.—"It is about two feet in length and looks as if it were part of a sleeve or stocking. In colour it is a dark brown and the material is woollen."

i. Several feeding-bottles of children. They were buried with them, and were probably filled with milk intended for their use.

j. A large bronze bowl 14in. in diameter, found at Malton in 1878.—*Exhibited by Mrs. Sellers.*

k. Two bronze lamps from York. The finest of them was found during the Railway excavations in 1876.

l. A small, elegantly-shaped, bronze vase, much corroded.

m. A pan or skillet of bronze, supposed to be a culinary vessel. Several vessels of this kind, found at Stittenham, are now preserved at Castle Howard.*—*From the Croft Collection,* 1824.

n. A part of another skillet found under the Exhibition Building, 1878.

o. A perforated, colander-shaped vessel found at Marston Moor.—*Mr. F. Bell,* 1860.

p. i. The sole of a Roman shoe.—*Railway Excavations,* 1875. ii. Sandal nails found in a stone coffin.—*Railway Excavations,* 1873.

q. A fine sandal, and a part of the stocking (?) of a Roman, of woollen, found among peat on a Moor near Ripon.— *Purchased at the sale of Mr. Stubbs, of Ripon,* 1878.

CASE N.

a. The boss of a Roman shield dredged up near the mouth of the river Tyne, 12in. long by 10in. broad, with a circular knob in the centre. The material is bronze coated with tin, and the figures, &c., have been made by scraping off the tin. On the central knob is carved the Roman eagle with a branch in its mouth. "In the corners we have representations of

---

* Two others were found at Swinton, near Masham. Engraved in Journal Arch. Inst. vi. 45-8. For an account of the vessels at Castle Howard, *cf.* Arch., xli. 325, &c.

the four seasons. Spring, in the upper left hand corner, is figured as a youth vainly striving, despite the winds of March, to gather his garments around him. A snake is seen at his feet, emerging from the ground, to indicate a renewal of vital energy in the lower creatures. Summer is represented in the opposite angle by a husbandman who grasps a scythe. Beneath the emblem of Spring we have the legend Leg. viii., and beneath that of Summer, Avg., the eighth legion having the name of *Augusta*. Below, we have Autumn, as a winged genius holding a huge bunch of grapes in the right hand, and a basket of corn or other fruits in the left. Winter, in the remaining corner, is clad in fur; the robe which hangs upon his arm is, as in the case of the Spring, made the sport of the winds."

" In the upper central compartment of the boss is a warrior in the attitude of attack, probably intended to represent Mars. In the corresponding compartment below, is a bull very spiritedly drawn. Above the bull is a crescent. The bull seems to have been the badge of the eighth legion."

" On the left hand margin of the plate is an inscription in punctured characters : which seems to be ɔ. IVL MAGNI IVNI DVBITATI ; the owners of the shield being in this case, Junius Dubitatus, of the century of Julius Magnus."*

The eighth legion was never in Britain, but Dubitatus, for some cause or other, seems to have visited this country, and probably lost his life in the Tyne. A portion of a helmet was found near the shield.

This is one of the choicest specimens of Britanno-Roman work in the country.—*Rev. William Greenwell*, 1876.

b. A large collection of bronze vessels, found near Knaresbrough, by some drainers ; they consist of a large urn,

* Dr. Bruce's Lapidarium Septentrionale, 58-9, where there is a fine plate o the shield, of which a copy is exhibited by its side.

12in. high ; one capacious dish, 19in. in diameter, which has
a hole in the centre for a pivot or screw; six basins of
graduated sizes ; a deep bowl with a crimped edge ; a dish to
which a long handle has been affixed; portions of seven
colanders perforated in patterns; a round plate ; the dish of a
small scale beam, with its rings for the chain ; four axe heads;
a spur ; and five large bronze rings. A number of other
vessels and implements were found at the same time, but were
unfortunately melted down without the cognizance of their
owner ; A bronze cup is still in the possession of the farmer
on whose land the discovery was made.*—*Mr. Thomas Gott,
of Knaresbrough,* 1864 and 1876.

CASE O.

The contents of this case consist chiefly of fragments of
white stone-ware *mortaria* and *amphorœ*. The entire vessels
of the first are bason or pan-shaped, of various capacity,
from one pint to a gallon, having the surface of the interior
studded like those of Samian ware, with small particles of
flint or quartz. One part of the rim is formed into a spout,
near which is generally stamped the name of the potter. Two
of these vessels are placed against the wall, which were found
in 1878 under the Exhibition. In each case the pestle has
at last found its way through. One of these mortars was
found on a Roman midden, and is stained by leaves and grass.

I. O. Handles, and curious fragments of vessels; part of
an urn with the head of a fawn on the side, similar to one in
the British Museum.

II. O. Fragments of vessels of white clay; frilled edges
of bowls ; bases of vessels showing how they were fitted on to
the body ; handles.

* Under this Case is a lead coffin, much decayed, found during the Railway
excavations.

III. O.   Parts of marble mortars ; pottery impressed with wooden stamps.

IV.—VI. O.   Parts of *mortaria*, of white or red ware, many of them showing the maker's name upon the edge.

Various parts of *amphoræ*.   *Amphoræ* were vessels used for holding olives, oil, honey, but especially wine : varying in size from six inches to three or four feet in height ; sometimes of a round shape, but generally tapering to a point or knob, so that it was necessary to place the bottom in a circular stand, or in sand, or some other yielding substance.   They are furnished with a short neck with two handles, whence their name is derived, on which, or on the rim of the neck, the maker's name was usually stamped.

VII.—XI. O.   Portions of the necks of large *amphoræ*, one of marble, and another from Lincoln with an inscription upon it in ink.

XII.—XVII. O.   Portions of *amphoræ* arranged to shew rims, handles, vases, potters' marks and necks.   On the rim is frequently scratched the number of *lagenæ*, or gallons, which the vessel contained ; an inscription in a cursive character upon the body of a vessel ; part of another inscription in deeply incised letters.

Case P.

a.   A round *ossuarium** of lead, 10½in. broad and 6in. high, with a little cupola with a handle on the top.   It is filled with burnt bones, and was found near the Holgate Railway Bridge.— *The Cook Collection*, 1872.

b.   The cupola and part of the body of another *ossuarium*, shaped like a Stilton cheese, 5in. high and 6in. wide.   It was found during the Railway excavations of 1846, in a large lead

* Engraved with the two following *Ossuaria* in C. R. Smith's Collect. Antiq. vii., pp. 172—6.

coffin, containing a skeleton. We may assume that the child had died first, and that its burnt bones were laid in its parent's coffin. With it were four fine vessels of glass.—*The Hargrove Collection*, 1847.

⁻ *c.* A large *ossuarium*, 15in. high by 10in., found in 1875, under the New Railway Station. It is unique in having the following inscription cut on it by a sharp-pointed tool—

D. M.

V(LP)IAE FELICISSIMAE

QVAE · VIXIT · ANNIS.

· III · MENSES · XI DIES.

· ·

F .... NT . VLPIVS . FELIX.

... ANDRONICA.

P. . . NTES.

The following are the contents of various Roman graves, kept apart by themselves.

d. A red, barrel-shaped cinerary urn, a small Samian cup with the lotus leaf on the rim, and a child's feeding bottle.— *Railway Excavations*, 1875.

e. A large Samian patera, with the lotus on the edge, and a dark fluted vessel.—*Railway Excavations*, 1872.

f. Two bowl-shaped vessels, a perfect one of glass, and another broken. Found at the head (outside) of a stone coffin, which contained the skeletons of two young girls.—*Railway Excavations*, 1873.

g. Two jugs and a large red lamp, out of which the wick* fell when it was being cleaned. It is of linen, and is exhibited. —*Railway Excavations*, 1875.

h. A black cinerary urn, with a small cup from the inside. —*Railway Excavations*, 1874.

i. A large red cinerary urn, with a lamp from the inside. —*Railway Excavations*, 1874.

---

* A bronze lamp with a wick in it was found at the Bartlow Hills, in 1840. *cf.* Arch. xxix. 4.

G

j. A black cinerary urn, fractured, preserved to show the collocation of the bones and ashes inside.—*The Mount,* 1874.

k. A large red jug and a black cinerary urn.—*Railway Excavations,* 1874.

l. A black cinerary urn. Inside it was a small black cup, a middle brass coin of Trajan, two enamelled *fibulæ* in the shape of ducks, and a fragment of a chain.—*Railway Excavations.*

m. A Samian bowl, and a black vessel with a cover, containing the bones of a dog.*

n. A fine black cinerary urn, and two beautiful vessels; a small glass jug, and a little black glazed cup with DAMI on it in white slip.

o. A small food vessel and a feeding bottle, from a child's grave.

p. A little brown cup found with three others, in a stone coffin near Severus' Place, on the Acomb Road.—*The Cook Collection,* 1872.†

CASE Q.

I. Q. *a.* A small piece of stucco from Tusculum. *b.* Stucco from Pompeii.—*Mr. Meynell,* 1823; *Mrs. Norcliffe.* *c.* Stucco from Aldborough.

II.—V. Q. Fragments of stucco, or wall plaster, found in 1831, near the interior of the Multangular Tower, and in 1873-6, during the Railway excavations. In one portion of the Roman cemetery a great quantity of plaster was found. It had evidently being carted thither out of the city.

VI. Q. Fragments of tessellated pavements found in York, chiefly from Toft Green. One or two pieces are from Acomb.

* The bones of a bird have been several times found in a food vessel at York.

† Under this Case is a small lead coffin of a child from the recent Railway excavations. The lid seems to have been a wooden board.

VII. Q. Portions of floor grouting, found under the City Wall, and in Aldwark.

VIII. Q. A stone ball, and the lid of a pot of red stoneware.

IX. Q. Perforated stones and pottery, and spindle whorls.

X. Q. Roundlets or discs of stone, probably children's playthings; whet-stones.

XI, XII. Q. Stone weights of various sizes, which have been slung on a cord or halter. Many of these have been found opposite St. Martin's Church in Micklegate. Two very large perforated stones are on the floor outside.—*Mr. E. Swaine, The Cook Collection, &c.*

XIII.—XIX. Q. A large series of bricks and tiles of the Ninth Legion, inscribed LEG IX HISP. (Legio nona Hispana). This Legion came into Britain with the Emperor Claudius, A.D. 44. In the beginning of the reign of Nero, it was nearly destroyed at Camulodunum (Colchester) by the forces of the British Queen Boadicea. It accompanied Agricola into the north, and there suffered greatly from the Caledonians. Returning southwards, it was stationed at York, where, in the reign of the Emperor Trajan, it was employed in the work commemorated by the tablet in the lower room of the Hospitium. On the arrival of the sixth legion, being reduced to the state of a weak legion, it is said to have been incorporated with it. This is more than doubtful, as the majority of the tiles exhibited here are long subsequent to the reign of Hadrian.

In XIV. Q. are the following stamped tiles—

a. Inscribed OPVS DOLIARE EX PRED. DOMINI AVG. denoting that the brick was made on a farm of the Emperor. In the centre is the brickmaker's mark, apparently a wolf.

b. Inscribed EXPRDPFLVCILLAE ODOL FEC MAPR LAEL CAES II P COEL BALBN COS ; *i.e.* EX PRÆDIO DOMITIÆ PUBLII FILIÆ LUCILLÆ OPUS DOLIARE FECIT M. APER LUCIO ÆL. CÆS. II P.

COEL. BALBIN. CONSULIBUS), denoting that the brick was made by Marcus Aper, on the farm of Domitia Lucilla, daughter of Publius, in the second consulship of Lucius Aelius (Verus) and the first consulship of Publius Coelius Balbinus, corresponding with A.D. 137. Domitia Lucilla was the daughter of Publius Calvisius Tullus. She was the wife of Annius Verus, and mother of the Emperor M. Aurelius.* The letters cos are in the centre, and above them a small palm branch, the maker's mark.—*Mr. Arthur Strickland, 1843.*

c. A fragment of a tile found at Slack, near Huddersfield, being a portion of a tile tomb, inscribed COH III BRE. The last word is variously interpreted, Professor Hübner considering it to be an abbreviation of Bretonum, *i.e.* Britons.—*Mr. Fairless Barber, 1869.* Another specimen of this stamp, also from, Slack.—*Mr. T. W. U. Robinson, 1879.*

CASE R.

A glass case filled with lamps, candlesticks, &c., found in York, and probably made there. No relics of ancient art are more numerous than lamps. They were used not only for domestic purposes, but in funeral solemnities. They were buried with the dead, and sometimes placed by relatives and friends on their tombs. From the situation in which the greater part of this collection was found, it is evident that they are sepulchral lamps. Lamps of terra-cotta are generally plain ; but they have occasionally figures on the top in bas-relief ; and the names of the makers are often stamped on the bottom. They are usually of an oval or of a round form, and those intended for domestic use are furnished with one or more nostrils, according to the number of wicks burned in them.

* Borghesi O. Epigr. i. 35.

Among these may be specially mentioned

a. Two large lamps of brown ware, said to have been found at Lincoln, but probably foreign.—*Mrs. Hutton*, 1848.

b. Two lamps, one with a female figure bearing a chaplet in her hand, near a column ; and another with a figure of a crocodile, on which Typhon (it is probable) the evil genius of the Egyptian mythology, is represented as standing. These two were found at Colchester.—*Mr. W. Whincopp*, 1847.

c. A lamp with three nostrils, found in the Roman baths at York.—*Mr. H. P. Cholmeley*, 1840.

d. Fragments of Candelabra.

e. A number of candlesticks of earthenware, of various shapes.

f. Several stands of lead and pot for holding lamps. Those of lead were generally suspended from the wall.

Under this Case is a lead coffin. It was found in 1868, near the Scarbro' Railway Bridge. A key was found upon the breast of the skeleton.

CASE S.

I.—VII. S. Bricks and tiles of the sixth legion ; inscribed LEG VI V. LEG VI VF. LEG VI V P F (Legio sexta victrix. Legio sexta victrix fidelis. Legio sexta victrix pia fidelis.) There are a few other unusual forms of inscription, which are probably instances of carelessness. The sixth legion came from Germany into Britain with the Emperor Hadrian, and after having been employed on his wall and that of Antoninus in Scotland, was stationed at York, which continued to be its head quarters as long as the Romans remained in Britain.

In I. S. are a number of small pipes of red clay, discovered in the Roman baths circa 1840, and connected, no doubt, with flues. Two or three round vessels of pot, with a small hole in them, probably intended to be filled with hot water, to warm the hands.

VIII.—XII. S. In these compartments are a few specimens of figured tiles called Antefixa ; used in ornamenting the exterior of dwelling-houses. They are of rude workmanship, and of very rare occurrence. Here are also two caps of flues, perforated as it were with windows ; and several objects of baked clay, the use of which it is not easy to conjecture.

XIII.—XVIII. S. These shelves exhibit a number of Roman bricks, one inscribed VR. SVS, the two first letters being ligulate and reversed ; others have patterns roughly scored on them ; flue-tiles, used in conveying heated air to baths and other rooms ; draining-tiles, which fit into one another in a very effective way. Against the wall are numerous other tiles and bricks, scored with dogs' feet, &c. One has the impressions produced by a heavy shower of hail which fell upon it when it was wet and unbaked.

CASE T.

I. T. *a.* Two tiles from Wells cathedral, 14th century. —*Rev. Greville Chester,* 1858.

b. Moorish tiles from Sidi Ben Medin, and Mansourah, near Tlemen in Algeria.—*Rev. C. B. Norcliffe,* 1878.

c. A large and richly ornamented tile from the Alhambra. —*Mr. W. Atkinson,* 1880.

d. A smaller tile from the same place with an inscription in Arabic.—*Rev. W. J. Waddilove.*

II. T. *a.* Four large tiles said to have come from the plateau of the high altar at Byland Abbey.—*The Hargrove Collection,* 1847.

b. Two tiles from a pavement which used to lie before the altar of St. Nicholas in York Minster. A small part of this pavement is now preserved in the vestry of the Minster, but most of the tiles found their way into Lincolnshire. An engraving of this pavement by Mr. W. Fowler, of Winterton, and presented in 1881 by his grandson, Rev. J. T. Fowler of Durham, is hanging on the wall.

c. Two late tiles from Watton Priory, E.R.Y.—*Purchased,* 1878.

d. Two plain tiles from the Priory of the Holy Trinity, Micklegate.

e. A tile from Gisborough Priory, bearing the arms of Kyme.—*Admiral Chaloner,* 1878.

f. Two tiles from Bridlington Priory, bearing the arms of Gilbert de Gaunt, the founder, with *Bridlington* around them.

III. T. *a.* Several small early tiles from Newminster Abbey, near Morpeth. *The Excavation Committee,* 1878.

b. Two early tiles from Meaux Abbey, Holderness, one bearing a fleur-de-lis.

c. Eight tiles from Salley Abbey in Craven. On one of them the words *Johe's Sallay abbas xps ihu,* have been written with a sharp pointed instrument when the clay was soft. On another is a large W enfiled by a crosier, commemorating another abbat.—*From the Walbran Collection,* 1870.

IV. T. Twenty-two tiles from Fountains Abbey, comprising, among others, many of those figured by Mr. Walbran in his description of the Excavations there. Among these is *a.* a compartment of plain tiles from the high-altar of thirteenth century work, if not earlier.—*From the sale of Mr. Stubbs of Ripon,* 1877. *b.* Six ornamented tiles set in a frame ; the kiln in which they were made was discovered near the abbey. *c.* The device of Marmaduke Huby, abbot, sæc. xv., consisting of a mitre pierced by a crozier, with the letters M. H. on the dexter side. Huby's motto *Soli Deo honor et gloria* runs around the shield.—*From Mr. Walbran's Collection,* 1870.

V. T. Three large ridge-tiles, formerly used on roofs.— *From St. Mary's Abbey.*

VI. T. *a.* A number of pieces of tiles, found in York, and ornamented with blue and yellow. Probably made in the sixteenth century.

b. A compartment of four tiles, set in a frame, and ornamented with oak leaves and acorns.—*Bought in York,* 1874.

VII. T. *a.* Tiles found in York.—*The Cook Collection,* 1872.

b. Four large tiles from St. Mary's Abbey.

VIII. T. Tiles from St. Mary's Abbey of various kinds, among these is a pattern of four tiles, each inscribed *Ave Maria.*

IX. T. *a.* Other tiles from St. Mary's chiefly of the 14th century, with several beautiful patterns.

b. A number of armorial tiles from St. Mary's Abbey. Among them are : *a.* A lion rampant crowned, *Darell.* *b.* France and England quarterly. *c.* or a plain cross sable, *Aton.* *d.* Chequy, *Warren.* *e.* Seven mascles, 3, 3, and 1, conjoined, *Quincy.* *f.* Two bars in chief three plates, *Colvill.* *g.* A fess between six cross crosslets, *Beauchamp.* *h.* A cross between four quatrefoils.

X. T. Some choice tiles from St. Mary's, many of which bear letters of the name of the patroness. There are also—

a. A tile found in the cloister of St. Mary's Abbey, having the alphabet in old English capitals inscribed upon it, and, with the exception of the second line, so arranged as to be read from right to left. Two fragments of similar tiles.

b. A tile of remarkable character, most probably one of a series representing the signs of the zodiac. It exhibits the figure of a ram, with the inscription,

SOL IN ARIETE (The sun in Aries).

From a more perfect specimen of one with the same device, and evidently formed by the same stamp, found in the ruins of Ulverscroft Priory in Charnwood Forest, it appears that the letters MAR were in the angles, denoting the month of March, in which the sun enters into that sign. It is supposed to have been fabricated in the fourteenth century.*

c. A tile bearing the following inscription in small Old English letters :—

Thenke-mon-thi-liffe
mai-not-eb-(ever) endure
that-thou-dost-thi-self
of-that-thow-art-sure
but-that-thow-kepist
unto-thi-settur-(executor's) cure
and-(an i. e. if) eb-hit-abail-the (thee)
hit-is-but-abenture

This remarkable tile is supposed to be one of the varieties of the tiles fabricated at Malvern. An engraved representation of it, but not a perfect fac-simile, was given by Dr. Nash, in his History of Worcestershire.†

d. A number of tiles found at Rossington, near Doncaster, in a place supposed to have been a domestic chapel of the Lords de Mauley, who are said to have resided there. Their date is probably the fourteenth century. Among them are these heraldic bearings.

a. On a bend sinister, three eagles displayed.—*Mauley.* *b.* A fess dancette between ten billets.—*Deincourt.* *c.* A fess vaire between three fleurs de lis.—*Cantilupe.* *d.* Seven mascles, 3, 3, and 1, conjoined.—*Quincy.* *e.* Lozengy.— *Fitzwilliam.*—*Mr. Henry Bower, of Doncaster,* 1889.‡

---

* *c.f.* Arch. Journal ii. 89; and a paper by Mr. James Fowler, in the Archæologia where this tile is engraved.

† See also Gent. Mag. for October, 1833, p. 301.

‡ *cf.* Journal, Arch. Ass., iv. 203.

XI. T. *a.* Four large wall tiles, ornamented with geometrical figures and foliage, found during the building of Parliament Street. Two of them have been filled originally with a white composition.—*The Hargrove Collection,* 1847. *b.* Several other tiles found in York.

XII. T. A number of tiles generally supposed to have been made in Holland, and largely used in fire places in England in the seventeenth and eighteenth centuries. Some of them are arranged in compartments of four each.— *Purchased in York.*

With the next compartment begins a remarkable collection of English earthenware vessels, of which the Society possesses a considerable number, and these very important and interesting in themselves. Nearly the whole of them have been discovered in York, and were purchased as they were found. As works of art they are very inferior to the fictile vessels of the Romano-British period, but they are of greater rarity. Being of little intrinsic value, and in constant daily use, comparatively few have escaped destruction. They are formed of a light-coloured, coarse clay, and are often covered, partially or entirely, with a green glaze. This was the popular colour for pottery in York, from the twelfth century to the eighteenth, and the ware was made in the city and its neighbourhood. It differs materially from the pottery found in London. North of York Mediæval vessels of this character are very rarely found. Cups and plates of wood, and pots and jugs of metal, must have taken their place, and the latter are often discovered.

A close examination of these vessels with the aid of Mediæval Inventories and Household Books, may perhaps ascertain most of the names which were ascribed to them. This work, however, has still to be done.*

* *cf.* Journal Arch. Inst. iii. 62, &c.; and the Lincoln Volume of the Institute xliii.; Journal Arch. Assoc., v. 22, &c.; C. R. Smith's Catalogue of his Museum,

On the top of the case is a large metal pot, with three legs, made about 1450, and purchased in York in 1877. Near it are some tall green-glazed vessels with holes in them for taps, and used probably for distilling. The large three-handled pot was found in the Bedern in 1873. The others are from villages near the city.

XIII. T. Some early jugs and vessels. One of them is a costrel, with a projection or ear on each side, through which a cord was passed, so that the vessel might be slung over the neck of the person who carried it, or suspended on a staff. The Museum contains other examples.

XIV. T. Several jugs with a glaze of light yellow, powdered with lead-coloured drops ; probably made in the thirteenth century.

XV. T. A large number of plain unglazed jugs, of a reddish ware, of frequent occurrence in York, and anterior, probably, to the fourteenth century.

XVI. T. Several large and very early jugs. One has four medallions or stamps on the sides, representing a man in combat with a dragon, a wheel near him, and a branch of a tree. We may ascribe this at least to the twelfth century. A very interesting jug, powdered with flowers, is near it. Near them are several stamps from the sides of vessels, resembling seals and a deer.

XVII. T. Cups, jugs, &c., of the fourteenth and fifteenth centuries. Among them is a brazier for burning charcoal, found at Lincoln. Conspicuous among its neighbours is a mutilated figure of St. Anthony and his pig, found in St. Mary's in 1858.

113, &c. In the Catalogue of the Bateman Museum are notices of some interesting vessels in it, which were found in York.

In every instance when the facts can be ascertained, the locality in which each piece of pottery in this case was found, and the date of its acquisition, is appended to it.

Two jugs of a bright green glaze, with a series of little
handles around them, with medallions or stamps, some of
which resemble Mediæval seals. The large jug in the centre
was found at the bottom of a well, and was presented by Lady
Macdonald in 1833. Near them are the mouths of some
vessels in the shape of the heads of grotesque animals, and the
handle of a vessel formed by two uncouth figures fastened to
the rim. The piece of pottery with the figure of a Saint
embossed upon it, was brought from Treves, by Miss H.
Crompton, and presented in 1874.

XVIII. T. Several rudely formed candlesticks.

XIX. T. A large jug and several tall narrow water vessels,
of the thirteenth and fourteenth centuries, all covered with
green glaze.

XX. T. A number of small jugs not later than the seventeenth century.

XXI. T. Three round vessels, found in the Multangular
Tower, and of a peculiar character. In the centre of one of
them there is a pillar on which is a dog's head ; in another
the head of a stag. These were drinking vessels, and the
circumference is divided into separate compartments, so that
when the cups were passed round the table each person might
have a distinct place from which to drink. On the head in the
centre was the crab or toast. Specimens of this kind of vessel
in silver are preserved in one or two of the colleges at Oxford.

XXII. T. A number of large and coarse vessels, among
which are some salt cellars ; a jug embossed with leaves ; a
pitcher with a frill around the rim and a hole for a tap ; and
a large vessel caught up from the bed of the Ouse off Bishopthorpe, at a depth of twenty feet, by a man who was creeping
for eels.

XXIII. T. A collection of jugs of various sizes, often
called Bellarmines, in derision of the Cardinal of that name.

They are covered with a mottled glaze; on the necks is a rudely bearded face; below this, very frequently, the arms of some town in Germany or Holland, where they were usually made. They were much used in England in the seventeenth century. Three of these were found in the Minster Yard in 1881, with the corks still in them.

A large yellow jug of Flemish or German work, sæe. xvi., with figures of Venus and Cupid embossed on it. Purchased at Harrogate.—*Mr. J. F. Walker*, 1872.

A brown German pitcher, dated 1581, and found in Clifton. The story of Susanna and the Elders is represented on it.— *Mr. V. Kitchingman*, 1882.

The greater part of a fine jug, sæc. 16th, ornamented with medallions, and with this inscription surrounding it: *Wein Got wil, so eist mein sil.*

On the top of the case are some smooth, unornamented vessels of the same class, which were in use in England after the Bellarmines.

XXIV. T. A number of costrels with a brown or black glaze, found in George Street in 1878, part of a large hoard laid three deep in a wooden rack or bin. With them were three small jugs of grey ware, and one or two others, with a portion of a plate. The date of these vessels must be between 1580 and 1610. The specimens from this find are kept together.—*Purchased*, 1878.

A number of small black cups or pots, some with two or more handles. They were used in the sixteenth and seventeenth centuries, and some of them are ornamented with yellow slip. They are frequently found in York in a fractured state. It is presumed that these are the vessels which in the reign of Elizabeth were called " black cruses," in the accounts of the Churchwardens of All Saints', Pavement.

Below are some fragments of chargers of tortoise shell ware which were in common use in the seventeenth century. There is a perfect specimen from York in the Bateman Museum at Sheffield.

XXV. T. A number of small vessels of various shapes, found in York, and made in the seventeenth and eighteenth centuries. Among them are two tygs, vessels surrounded with diminutive handles, more for ornament than for use.

XXVI. T. Jugs of green or brown ware made in or near York in the beginning of the last century. With them are two net-weights of baked clay, taken from the bed of the Ouse.

Under the centre of this long Case is a large collection of vessels in stone, or stone ware, consisting chiefly of mortars and creeing troughs, from the fourteenth century downwards, several of which are dated. There are also crucibles of stone and pots of various shapes and sizes.

XXVII.—XXXII. T. In these compartments and on the top of the Case is a continuation of the pottery which has been already described. The series extends from the sixteenth to the eighteenth century, and contains some interesting specimens. Among them are examples of what is called Fulham ware, two of which were presented in 1873, by Mr. J. F. Walker. Of early white ware there are several examples, including a triplet of flower cups, probably of the date of Charles I. A white jug for claret, dated 1644. A small cup bought at Ripon in 1878, which bears the head of Charles II; and several two-handled vessels for distilling herbs. A pipkin of early French work, was presented by Dr. Sykes, of Doncaster, in 1874. Of brown ware, ornamented with yellow or plain, there are several specimens, especially puzzle jugs. There are some early chargers, about 14in. in diameter, on one of which is a youth with a spear, resembling Prince Henry, brother of Charles I, bought at Beverley, in 1880. On another, of early Staffordshire work, are St. George and the Dragon. These vessels were usually the decorations of old oak chests or cabinets. Upon each vessel is a label stating where it was acquired.

XXXIII.—XXXVII. T. A representative collection of drinking glasses and bottles, the contents of the three upper shelves being a loan from a private collector, with the exception of a bottle from Whixley manor house, sæc. 17, of Dutch work, with this inscription : *Concerning Constancy—It is a hidden treasure.* This bottle was shown in 1857, at the Manchester Exhibition.

The glasses with white stalks were largely used in this country down to the beginning of the present century. They were made chiefly in Holland, or by Dutch glass-makers, who settled in England, especially at Newcastle-on-Tyne. The art of making them has been recently recovered and revived.

On the two lower shelves is a collection of glass bottles of various shapes and sizes, made in the seventeenth and eighteenth centuries, all of them from the neighbourhood of York. It was customary to affix to the side of the bottle a little roundlet of glass bearing the owner's name, or arms. Of this practice we have several examples. One bottle, found in York, and from the Hargrove collection, has $\frac{M}{T.M.}$ stamped upon it ; another has the arms of Peirson, of Lowthorpe, in the East Riding ; a third, *Castle Howard*, 1753.

In the windows are placed specimens of the glass-painting of Giles and Peckitt, two famous glaziers in York, in the seventeenth and eighteenth centuries.

IV.

ANTIQUITIES IN THE HALL, THEATRE, AND UPPER ROOM OF THE MUSEUM.

The Hall contains, besides antiquities, two modern busts; one, by Chantrey, of the Rev. Wm. V. Harcourt, the first President of the Society; the other, by Leyland, of Halifax, of the late Stephen Beckwith, M.D., to whom the Society is indebted for a munificent legacy of ten thousand pounds.*

No. I. On the left hand side entering. This case contains two pieces of Egyptian sculpture. The uppermost is a *stele*, or funeral tablet, of the sandstone of Upper Egypt. It represents "PETAMON, a distributor of libations," performing a *proscynema*, or act of adoration, to Osiris Pethempamenthes, Lord of Abydos. Osiris, wearing the royal cap of Upper Egypt, is standing on a square base, and holding his usual emblems, the hook and flail or scourge. Before him is an altar, on which stands a water-vase and the flower of a water-plant. Petamon is in an attitude of adoration; on his arm hangs a bag, supposed to be a seed-bag, and, like the hoe and flail, to have a reference to the employment of the deceased in the Elysian Fields. The hieroglyphics at the base record a peace-offering made to Osiris, including flesh of geese and oxen, linen, incense, and wax. Over the heads of the figures is the winged disc of the sun, and below it six columns of hieroglyphics, which are an abridgment of the inscription at the base.

In the lower part of this case are contained fragments of sandstone, on which the names of the gods Osiris Pethempamenthes, Ra (the solar disc) and Athom or Atmoo are

inscribed : but its original purpose cannot be ascertained.—
Col. Vernon Harcourt, 1830.

No. II. A cast of an Assyrian tablet cut upon the face of
a rock on the coast of the Mediterranean Sea, on the south
side of the mount of the Nahr-el-Kelb, near Beyrout. It is
one of ten ancient monuments sculptured on the rock at
different heights, and at various periods. The most ancient
are three Egyptian ; the next in antiquity are five Assyrian or
Chaldæan, the highest and most perfect of which is represented
in this cast, taken under the direction of Mr. Joseph Bonomi.
It exhibits the figure of a man in the dress of the eastern
nations, with a large beard curiously plaited, holding in his
right hand something like a fan, or, as Mr. Landseer supposes,
a dove ; " and in his left hand a stick," or staff-sceptre.
Nearly the whole of the background and dress of the figure is
covered with an inscription in Assyrian cuneiform characters,
in some places well preserved, but generally very indistinct.
This tablet represents Esarhaddon, who invaded Egypt and
Ethiopia, b. c. 673, and inscribed the rock on his return.*—
Mr. Joseph Bonomi, 1837.

No. III. A stele of the limestone of Lower Egypt. It
consists of three compartments. In the uppermost the
deceased, a royal scribe, performs a *proscynema* to Osiris, who
is seated, Isis and Nephthys standing behind him. The
deceased offers incense and pours a libation to the god ; on the
table before him are a cake and the flower of a water plant.

In the second compartment, the deceased appears seated
between his parents ; before them is a conventional representation of trees, the emblem of Ammon-Khem. His son and
widow are making offerings ; the latter has the funeral cone
(see p. 45, No. 66) on her head.

* Trans. of the Royal Soc. of Lit., 4to., vol. ii., p. 105. Journal of Royal Asiatic
Soc., vol. x., pt. 1, p. 27.

In the third compartment, the deceased and his wife are seated together, receiving the homage of their children, a son and two daughters. A table before them has on it a cake and flowers; the son offers incense. This sculpture is from Mr. Salt's Collection.—*Mr. John R. Mills*, 1835.

No. IV. On the floor is a cast, made by Mr. Joseph Bonomi, of one of the great obelisks at Karnak, the eastern part of Thebes, erected by Amense, sister to Thothmes II., in the name of her husband Amenenthituot, whose shield is seen near the bottom. On the apex or *pyramidion* Ammon Ra seated, places his hand, as a sign of inauguration, on the head of the king. The central line of hieroglyphics records that Amenenthituot had erected two obelisks before the gate of Ammon.* The sculptures in the eight compartments besides the central line represent the god Ammon Ra receiving various offerings; in the uppermost he is embracing the sovereign. The other three sides of the obelisk are covered with sculptures and inscriptions similar to this.—*George Goldie, M.D.*

No. V. A cast of the famous black obelisk from Nimroud, discovered by Mr. Layard, and now in the British Museum.— *Rev. J. Kenrick*, 1870.

No. VI. The mortar of the Infirmary of the Abbey of St. Mary. It is of bell-metal, weight seventy-six pounds, and bears the following inscription : On the upper rim,—

+MORTARIU. SCI. JOHIS. EUANGEL. DE. IFIRMARIA. BE. MARIE. EBOR.

The lower+FR. WILELS. DE. TOUTHORP. ME. FECIT. AD. MCCCVIII.†

---

* Bosellini Mon. Stor. 3, 1, 152.

† Mortarium Sancti Johannis Evangelistæ de Infirmaria Beatæ Mariæ Ebor. Frater Willielmus de Touthorp (a village near York) me fecit, Ao. D. MCCCVIII

Of the history of this beautiful specimen of mediæval art, during nearly two centuries after the dissolution of the Abbey, nothing is known.   Tho earliest notice we have of it occurs in an anonymous letter to Gent, published by him in his History of Hull, and dated 1734 ; from which it appears that, after having been long in the possession of the Fairfax family, it had passed into the hands of Mr. Smith, a bell-founder in York, by whom it had been sold to Mr. A. Addington, in the custody of whose son, a confectioner (Drake says—Eboracum, p. 583—a perfumer) in the Minster Yard, it was seen by the writer of the letter.   Gough, in the translation of Camden's Britannia, published in 1789, says, (vol. iii. p. 66,) "it was lately in the hands of an apothecary at Selby; after whose death all traces of it were lost."   In the year 1811, it was discovered by Mr. Rudder, a bell-founder at Birmingham, amidst a large quantity of old metal, which he had probably purchased from York or the neighbourhood.   Unwilling to commit so beautiful a relic to the furnace, he put it aside year after year, and finally presented it to his antiquarian friend Mr. Blount, an eminent surgeon in Birmingham. After his death it was sold by auction, in the year 1835, and purchased at a considerable price by Mr. S. Kenrick, who restored it to its proper place among the remains of the religious establishment to which it originally belonged.

The stand is formed* of oak, taken from the roof of the North Transept of the Minster, when undergoing repair, after a pattern in one of the centre bosses of the vaulting of the Nave, representing the Annunciation, destroyed in the last fire.† The vaulting of the North Transept, and the carving of the boss, were nearly coeval with the casting of the mortar.

On the other side are some Roman sculptures which have been already described among the contents of the Lower Room in the Hospitium, to which the visitor must refer. They consist of the fine statue attributed to Mars, but which Mr. W. T. Watkin conceives may represent Britannia, (No. 12, in the Catalogue); the sarcophagus of Julia Fortunata (No. 44); the Mithraic sculpture (No. 19); the figure of Eternity (No. 1); the monument of Ælia Æliana (No. 45); and altars to Mars (No. 11); the Matres Domesticæ (No. 15); and the Deus Vetus (No. 24). On another ledge are small altars dedicated to Fortune (No. 4); the Deæ Matres (No. 16); and another inscription to the Deus Vetus (No. 23).

In the Theatre. The Case on the right hand contains some portions of plate and chain armour, swords, and other weapons, &c. Here also are deposited the singular fetters which were formerly exhibited at York Castle, consisting of those worn by Nevison and Dick Turpin, the famous Highway-

* By the direction and at the expense of the Rev. C. Wellbeloved.
† See Browne's History of the Metropolitan Ch. of St. Peter, York, plate xcvi.

men ; a set found in the Castle Moat on the legs of a skeleton, discovered in 1773, and supposed to be a prisoner of the name of William Thompson, who had been missing for twenty years ; also a sample of the fetters which, until the beginning of this century, were placed upon every criminal committed to gaol, the weight of the shackles corresponding to the heinousness of the offence charged against him. The branding iron is also here, and the thumb screw as well. In a corner is one of those murderous weapons, a spring-gun, bought in 1881, from Knaresbrough ; and appended to the wall, is a brank, the old punishment for scolding women, given by Lady Mary Thompson, late of Sheriff-Hutton Park, in 1880.

The Case on the left hand of the door is filled with a collection of pottery, &c., from Cyprus and Crete, deposited for exhibition by Mr. T. B. Sandwith, C.B., Her Majesty's Consul in Crete.

The three tapestry maps upon the walls of the Theatre, formerly lined the Hall at Weston, in Warwickshire, the seat of W. Sheldon, Esq., who introduced tapestry weaving into England, of which these maps, executed in 1579, are the first specimens. They contain a section of the centre of the kingdom, including Herefordshire, Shropshire, Staffordshire, Worcestershire, Warwickshire, Gloucestershire, Oxfordshire, and part of Berkshire. They were purchased by the Earl of Orford, (Horace Walpole,) and given by him to Earl Harcourt.* On his death they came into the possession of Archbishop Vernon Harcourt, by whom they were presented to the Yorkshire Philosophical Society, in the year 1827.

The Coins in the possession of the Society are placed in the Council Room. Shortly after the establishment of the Society, a collection of about 1200 Roman and English coins was

---

* See Nichols's Literary Anecdotes, vol. viii. 2nd Series, p. 686. Several others of the same series are in the Bodleian library.

purchased of the late Mr. Henwood, of York, chiefly by means
of a liberal private subscription. A considerable number was
added by the purchase of the late Mr. Hargrove's collection,
and other purchases have been occasionally made of coins
found in York or the neighbourhood. Some, not previously
possessed by the Society, have been added from the recent
Railway excavations. Donations of varied extent and value
have also been presented to the Society. In a collection thus
formed there must be many repetitions, and many deficiencies.
It contains, however, much that is curious and valuable. It
consists chiefly of Roman denarii, consular and imperial; of
Roman brass of three sizes; and of English coins, in silver
and copper of all denominations. Of Greek coins there are
very few; of Roman aurei very few; and the number of
English gold coins is not large. Of ancient British and Saxon
coins there are several rare and interesting examples. The
most extensive and complete portion of the collection is a series
of Northumbrian stycas, consisting of about 4,000 of the hoard
found in St. Leonard's Place, York, in 1842, and of about
2,000 of that which was discovered in 1847, near Bolton
Percy.*

The Society possess also a considerable number of modern
foreign coins, in silver and copper; and some tradesmen's
tokens; some jettons and Nuremberg counters : some medals,
foreign and English; and numerous impressions of seals, in
plaster, sulphur, and wax.

This portion of the Museum is necessarily kept under lock
and key; but it may be inspected by any member of the
Society, or any visitor introduced by a member, on application
to the Curator of the Antiquities.

* The remainder of the coins in this find was purchased for Mr. Thos. Bateman,
by Mr. Robert Cook.

THE STAIRCASE.

On the wall, as you pass towards the Ethnological Room, are several portraits, the majority of which have been recently removed from the Entrance Hall to escape the damaging effect of the light and dust. At the foot of the staircase are the portraits of three York musicians, Dr. Camidge, the organist of the Minster, in crayons; and Philip Knapton, senior and junior; two of which were placed here on the dissolution of the York Musical Society. As you climb the stairs you see a cluster of portraits, all representing men of note in the antiquarian world, or gratefully remembered by the Society. The series begins with a small, indifferent picture of Francis Drake, the historian of York, presented by Mr. Richard Roundell, in 1830; next in sequence comes Thomas Beckwith, F.S.A., painter and antiquary, delineated by himself; after him is a likeness of John Phillips, F.R.S., the first keeper of the Museum, and a man whom, whether in life or death, the Society has been proud to honour, this picture was presented by Mr. R. Davies, in 1874; next, we have James Atkinson, one of the founders of the Society, painted by Etty, and presented in 1857, by his daughter, Lady Chatterton; another specimen of Etty's skill is near, in the faithful likeness of John Brook, attorney-at-law, which belonged to the York Musical Society; the series ends with the portraits of two distinguished scholars, related in tastes and kinship, to whom the Society is greatly indebted; Charles Wellbeloved, curator of antiquities from 1823 to 1858; and John Kenrick, his learned son-in-law, who took up his relative's post, and died in 1877 at the great age of 89. Mr. Wellbeloved's likeness is by Lonsdale, and was presented in 1859; the painter of Mr. Kenrick's portrait was George Patten. It came to the Society in 1880, through the bequest of his widow. In the Council room is a fine bust

in lead, of Thomas, Lord Fairfax, which was acquired by the
Society by purchase in 1879. It had been long preserved in
the family of Thompson, at Sheriff-Hutton Park, having probably belonged to the Ingrams, the earlier possessors of that
estate, who were connected by marriage with the great
Parliamentary General.

V. THE ETHNOLOGICAL ROOM IN THE MUSEUM.

In this room are deposited the British and Anglian antiquities which the Society possesses, together with a large
miscellaneous collection of English curiosities of a comparatively recent date. This room will also contain a small
collection of Egyptian antiquities which has hitherto been
placed in the Hospitium, but is not yet properly classified.

The objects in flint and stone are for the most part the
collection of the late Mr. Charles Monkman, of Malton, which
the Society acquired by purchase in 1875. These implements
and weapons are divided according to their antiquity into
Palæolithic and Neolithic.

Case A.

I. A. i. A small set of casts of implements of carved
bone discovered in the Dordogne caves, representing *inter
alia* the deer and the mammoth.—*The Trustees of the Christy
Collection*, 1867. ii. A few flints and bones from the same
source.

II.—IV. A. Numerous wrought flints collected by the
Rev. W. Greenwell, from the Drift gravel pits at Icklingham,
Warren Hill, Santon-Downham, &c., in Suffolk.

V. A.   A few flints from the Drift gravel in the valleys of the Somme and Seine.*—*M. Boucher de Perthes*, 1860, &c.

VI.—X. A.   A number of Neolithic implements in flint and stone from Denmark and Sweden.   Many of those from Sweden were the gift of Rev. J. Raine, in 1875.

XI.—XX. A.   A very large collection of axes, adzes, axe-hammers,† pounders, knives, arrow-heads, scrapers, &c., &c., almost entirely from the Yorkshire Wolds, and gathered together for the most part by Mr. Monkman.‡

Among these, in XVII. A., is a small hoard of flint and stone axes and knives found in 1868, in sand, near the Gas Works of the North Eastern Railway.‖   Some of these were the gift of Mr. E. Allen, in 1870.   In XII. A. is a magnificent round flint knife, found near Catton.

XXI.—V. A.   Numerous flint and stone implements, &c., from Antrim, Toome, and Lough Neagh, in Ireland, acquired by purchase, and from the Monkman Collection.§

XXVI. A.   A small collection of implements and weapons in obsidian from Mexico, said to have been used by the Aztecs. —*Presented by a donor who wishes to be nameless*, 1880.

XXVII. A.   Some fine weapons, &c., from New Zealand, several of them in jade.

XXVIII.—IX. A.   A collection of stone axes, pounders, knives, arrow-heads, &c., from North America.   The smaller

---

* *cf.* Archæologia, xxxviii., 280, &c.

† The best work of reference on this subject is that by Mr. John Evans, F.S.A. A few of the flints in the Museum were found near Bridlington, and were presented by Mr. Barugh, in 1869.

‡ In the drawers in the Hospitium are some admirable counterfeits of these implements, made by Flint Jack, which are well worthy of preservation. Several specimens of these forgeries were presented by Mr. Ruddock, of Whitby, in 1857; and by Mr. T. M. Kendal, of Pickering.

‖ *cf.* Journal of Yorkshire Topographical and Archæological Society, part i. pp. 47—61.

§ *cf.* Archæologia, xli., 397, &c.

H

objects were chiefly presented by Mr. Joseph Clark, of Cincinnati, in 1851.

XXX. A. Some cores and flakes of flint, of the Palæolithic period, from Pressigny in France.*—*Mr. John Evans, F.S.A.,* 1865.

On the floor of the large Case, below, are four coffins of wood, formed by splitting the trunks of oaks longitudinally, and very rudely shaped. They are of the Anglian, or Anglo-Saxon period, and were used by persons in a humble position of life.

i. This was found in excavating for the foundation of Salem Chapel, in St. Saviourgate, and seems to have contained the body of a fisherman or boatman, a portion of a paddle having been found in the coffin, where it still remains. The coffin appears to have been fastened together by wooden pegs. The bottom of the coffin was in great decay and was replaced by another more perfect found in Parliament Street.†—*The Hargrove Collection,* 1847.

ii. A coffin of a similar character, but more rude, enclosing the skeleton of a female, and found in the Church Hill, Selby, not far from the Ouse, some eight feet below the present surface, with many others. The coloured beads represented in the drawing were discovered in it.‡ On the summit of the skull is a small round hole, apparently drilled, which has not up to this time been satisfactorily explained. The same thing has been observed in a Roman skull, discovered during the recent Railway Excavations.—*Mr. C. T. Newstead,* 1861.

* cf. Archæologia, xl., 381, &c., for a paper by Mr. Evans, on these flints.

† In November, 1878, several roughly shaped coffins of oak were found in Parliament Street, under the shop of Messrs. Makins and Dean, some twelve feet below the level of the street. They were broken up by the workmen, and only a single skull was brought to the Museum. There has been no cemetery in this place during historic times.

‡ These have been unfortunately destroyed. They were given to a child who ground them down upon the kitchen floor.

iii. iv.   Two similar coffins found with many others at the same place in 1876.   A long account of this find is given in the Report of the Society for that year.   At the head of one of these coffins was found a stout head post of oak, which stands in the Case as it was found.   In both of these coffins rods and branches of hazel were discovered, some fragments of which are exhibited.   They were probably intended to serve as charms.—*Messrs. Morrell, Atkinson, and Woods*, 1876.

On the top of the Case is an ancient British canoe, dug up in 1838, from the bed of the Calder, at Stanley Ferry, near Wakefield.   It was found at the depth of 18ft. 6in. below the present surface of the ground, and about 6 feet below the ordinary bed of the river.   Its dimensions were about 17ft. 9in. in length, and, in its widest part, 3ft. 10in., inward measure.   It is formed entirely out of one tree, and without any appearance of iron about it.*   Many large oak trees, quite black and sound, were found near it.—*Mr. George Bankes*, 1840.

CASE B.

I. B.   A small collection of British pottery.   The British urns are of rude workmanship, being formed by the hand, without the aid of the wheel or lathe ; and being merely sun-baked, or slightly reddened by fire on the outside, are very fragile.   They are found chiefly in barrows.   They are generally divided into cinerary urns, food vessels, and incense cups.   Among these may be noted.

i.   A cinerary urn, 19in. high, the finest that has been found in Yorkshire, discovered in the centre of a barrow at Bishop Burton, near Beverley, about two feet below the surface of the adjoining ground, with the mouth upwards, and filled

---

* There is a notice of it, with a cut, in Bowman's Reliquiæ Ebor., p. 40.   *cf.* Arch. xxvi., 257, &c., for an account of a similar canoe found at North Stoke.

with earth above the ashes.   Some armlets were found with it.
—*Dr. Hull, of Beverley*, 1827.

ii.   A fine drinking cup, found in Bootham in 1840, when the York and Scarbro' Railway was being made.

iii.   A prettily ornamented food vessel, with a stone axe, found at Norton, near Malton.

iv.   A remarkable, cup-shaped vessel with a large handle, found at Danes Graves, near Pocklington, and presented by Mr. Thomas Smith, of Huntington Hall, in 1825.

The remaining vessels, with the exception of one found at Rigg, and presented by Mr. G. H. Seymour, in 1844, were disinterred by the York Antiquarian Club, and presented to the Society in 1849.   A minute account of these excavations is preserved in the Council room,* in the Register of the Antiquarian Club which was drawn up by its Secretary, Dr. Procter.

II. B.   This compartment contains a very remarkable series of articles of the Early Iron and Late Celtic period, discovered by the Rev. E. W. Stillingfleet, in the barrows at Arras and Hessleskew on the Wolds, consisting of a portion of an urn and jet necklace belonging, probably, to the Bronze period; tires of wheels, a bridle-bit, parts of horse trappings, armlets, *fibulæ*, rings, and other ornaments and implements of iron and bronze, belonging to the Early Iron period;† beads of white and blue, and green and white glass, of the same period.

Mr. Stillingfleet and a friend made these explorations and unfortunately divided the results.   They discovered, among others, two interments in which the chief had been interred with his war chariot, of these each discoverer took a wheel.

* *cf.* Journal Arch. Assn., v. 369—370; Bowman's Reliquiæ Antiquæ, 38—39.

† In the Archæologia, xvi., 348, is a description with plates of some antiquities found at Hagbourn Hill, Berks, some of which are very similar to these.

The many interesting objects found were severed in the same ruthless manner. Mr. Stillingfleet ensured the safety of his share by presenting it to this Museum, in 1865. The other half has been missing until recently, when it most unhappily came into the possession of the British Museum. The interest of the collection is thereby entirely destroyed. The two odd chariot wheels which the British Museum has acquired are exhibited as if they came from one place, which is not the case.

III. B. A small collection of bronze implements and weapons, in which most of the usual forms are represented.* Among these are the early flat axe, socketed celts, paalstabs, chisels, gouges, swords, daggers, and spears. A few may be mentioned.

i. Four bronze swords found in Holderness.—*The Monkman Collection*, 1875.

ii. A part of a large hoard of celts, found at Westow, near Malton, and purchased in 1845.

iii. Some chisels and gouges found in Lincolnshire.

iv. With these is a piece of coarse woollen cloth discovered by Mr. Stillingfleet, in a barrow on Skipwith Common, in 1817.

The locality in which each implement was found is carefully appended to the object, whenever it is known, but in many instances this information is unfortunately missing.†

IV. B. This compartment contains a typical collection of the objects found in various places in Switzerland, which

* *cf.* Arch. Journal, iv., 1, 327; vi., 363 ; Journal Arch. Assn., iii., p. 58; and, above all, Mr. John Evans's recent work on the subject.

† The following extracts from the *Liber Donorum* show how the advent of these curiosities was recorded:—1823, a celt from the Isle of Axholme, presented by Rev. J, Graham; 1823, a celt found at Stittenham, presented by Mr. R. Tuke; 1827, a celt, presented by Lieut.-General Sharpe ; 1830, a celt from Rudgate, pres. by R. Brogden, Esq.; 1838, an antique brass spear-head, found near Whitestone Cliff, presented by C. H. Elsley, Esq.; 1844, a celt, presented by Dowager Duchess of Leeds ; 1847, five celts, presented by Mr. Whincopp.

either are or have been lakes, such as Wangen, Möringen, Locraz, Sutz, and the Lake of Bienne. They are the relics of Celtic tribes which occupied houses of wood built upon large wooden frames, a little above the level of the lakes· These peculiar residences were chosen to ensure protection from foes. The floor of the lake below became gradually strewn with various objects which had fallen from above. Some traces of these remarkable dwellings* have been found in Ireland, Scotland, and Wales.—*Purchased*, 1876, *etc.*

CASE C.

I. C. *a*. A large and miscellaneous collection of Anglian ornaments and weapons, some of which were found at Kilham and presented by the Rev. E. W. Stillingfleet in 1865 ; others are from a mound at Driffield, which was opened by Mr. R. Jennings,† and the York Antiquarian Club in 1845 ; a few are from an Anglian cemetery at Londesbrough, and were presented by Lord Londesbrough in 1880. The *fibulæ* and beads are worthy of special observation.

b. A large *umbo* and handle of a shield,‡ etc., found in a tumulus at Sowerby, near Thirsk, with a quantity of Roman pottery (which is preserved in a drawer in the Hospitium) by the York Antiquarian Club.—*Lady Frankland Russell*, 1855.

c. A very remarkable collection of ornaments, implements, and weapons, found in a grave-mound at Uncleby, in the parish of Kirkby Underdale, E.R.Y. Among them are brooches and *fibulæ* of gold and silver ; also a lady's box‖ con-

---

* The best account of them is in " The Lake Dwellings of Switzerland and other parts of Europe, by Dr. Ferdinand Keller. Translated by John Edward Lee. 2 vols. 8vo, London, 1878."

† There is an account of Mr. Jennings's discoveries in the Journal of the Arch. Assn., ii. 55—6. Many of the objects are figured in Akerman's Pagan Saxondom.

‡ Mr. C. R. Smith's Inventorium Sepulchrale, pl. xv.

‖ Similar objects may be seen in the Inventorium Sepulchrale, pl. 13.

taining the thread, undecayed, and some fine swords and iron implements.—*Rev. W. Greenwell*, 1874.

d. A finely fluted glass bowl, found on the Mount, where there was an Anglian cemetery.

e. A cup or basin formed of two thin plates of metal, one silver, the other copper, both gilded. The exterior, or silver plate, is ornamented with a pattern, in relief, of foliage and fruit, which birds are devouring. On the rim, which is of curious work, have been four beads of coloured glass or paste, one of which is remaining. The interior, or gilded copper plate, is plain ; but to the bottom an elegant circular piece of work is affixed, of about ¼in. in thickness, and 2½ in. in diameter, in which have been four bosses or studs of coloured glass or paste, which appear to have been surrounded by a circle of sixteen pearls, one of which is remaining. Between the four bosses is an interlaced pattern of gilded wire, delicately marked, so as to resemble rope work. A similar interlaced pattern, in relief and plain, is seen on the outside of the bowl, between four short feet on which it is supported. This noble relic, one of the finest known specimens of Anglo-Saxon workmanship, was found in the churchyard of Ormeside, in Westmerland.—*Mr. John Bland, of Ormside Lodge*, 1823.

f. A silver armlet, found in a field at Flaxton,* near Lobster-house, on the road to Malton. Probably found in 1807. From the Collection of Mr. John Croft.—*Rev. R. Croft*, 1824.

g. A silver *fibula,* enclosing within a series of concentric circles, a cast of a silver coin of the Emperor Valentinian. From the Croft Collection.—*Rev. R. Croft*, 1824.

h. A gold coin of the Emperor Arcadius with a loop affixed

* This is very similar in shape and design to some ornaments found at Cuerdale, which are figured in the Journal Arch. Inst., iii. 116, which are supposed to date from the year 900. They are Eastern in character. See also the Catalogue of the National Museum at Edinburgh, pp. 110—11. A number of St. Peter's pennies, etc., were found at Flaxton at the same time. *cf.* Gent. Mag. for the year.

to it, and used as a pendant. It was found near Newbuilding. *Mr. C. H. Elsley*, 1838.

i. A small Anglian *fibula* in lead, found in York, and engraved in the Journal of the Arch. Association, ii. 312. *The Hargrove Collection*, 1847.* A small mould in stone for making these *fibulæ*, is beside it. It was recently found in York.

j. An oval seal (?) of copper, engraved like a bracteate, with horses heads and other ornamentation, but obscured by encrustation. Found in College Street.—*Tempest Anderson, M.D.*, 1881. A small Danish seal of brass with a head and legend, an imitation of a Saxon coin.—*The Hargrove Collection*, 1847.

k. A set of amber beads from Exning, near Newmarket.— *Mr. W. Whincopp*, 1847.

l. A bead, and a piece of bronze plating, found with the coffins of wood at Selby.

m. Various objects discovered in York, among which are a girdle-hanger,† and a fine bronze pin.

n. A copper dish, with patches, found in digging a drain in St. Saviourgate.—*Rev. John Graham*, 1835.

o. Another copper dish, of the same period, with interlacing work, found in excavating for the Gaol in the Castle Yard.—*Mr. W. Fenton Scott*, 1829.‡

p. Several small objects ; i., a small pendant cross, ornamented with circles, found in Pavement, 1879 ; ii., an ornament for holding a knitting needle, of deer's horn, found near Micklegate Bar, 1881 ; iii. and iv., two small, prettily carved brooches, one found in York in 1877, the other at Naburn in the same year and presented by *Mr. G. Kidd.*||

* *cf.* Mr. C. R. Smith's Catalogue of his Museum, p. 106, for another example.
† *cf.* Smith's Inventorium Sepulchrale, pref. xiv. and p. 8 ; Arch. Journal, vi. 20
‡ Similar objects are described and engraved in Mr. C. R. Smith's Account of the Faussett Collection.
|| In Bowman's Reliquiæ Antiquæ, p. 9, there is a cut of a curiously ornamented object in bone from York, now in the Bateman Collection.

q. A large and fine series of Anglian or Danish combs, buckles, etc., from York, several having interlacing ornaments upon them. One of these is a comb-case, on which there is the beginning of the only Runic inscription that has been found in York.* Another is a fragment of bone, presented by Mr. R. Davies, and found in his garden, on which an English carver seems to have modelled some of his ornaments.†

r. Several Anglian or Danish swords and spears. One of them was found in the bed of the Ouse, near Kelfield, and was presented by Mr. Wm. Gray.

s. Six Anglian urns and a small bottle,‡ found on the Mount, filled with burnt bones.—*Mr. F. Calvert and Mr. E. Rooke*, 1859—60.

t. Several similar urns, said to have been found at Broughton, near Malton, circa 1802, and to have been bought by Sir Mark Masterman Sykes.—*Rev. Chr. Sykes*, 1823.

CASE D.

The upper part of this Case is entirely filled with a large series of Anglian urns, discovered in 1878, a little to the East of York, near the suburb of Heworth. They are funereal, and contained ashes and burnt bones, and were laid in rows athwart a ridge of ploughed land, some two feet apart. Several of them contained beads fused by heat ; one, a pair of fine bronze tweezers ; another, some buttons. When found, they were in many pieces, but the skill and patience of the late Dr. Gibson made them what they are. This is the

---

* This is figured and described by Professor Stephens of Copenhagen, in the *Illustreret Tidende,* and will also appear in the forthcoming Volume of his Runic Monuments.

† Compare these with plate xv. in the Inventorium Sepulchrale of the Faussett Collection and with Akerman's Pagan Saxondom, pl. xxxi.

‡ *cf.* Inventorinm Sepulchrale, pref. xv. ; and Journal Arch. Assn., where there is a cut of an exactly similar vessel found in Warwickshire.

H 2

largest series of Anglian vessels hitherto found in any one place.
They may probably be ascribed to the 5th or 6th century.

I. D. *a*. Ancient skates, formed of the leg-bones of horses,
polished on one side. They are frequently found in York, as
at London and Lincoln, and were probably introduced into
England by the Danes.* They are mentioned in a description
of the sports of the citizens of London, by a writer in the time
of Henry II.

b. A pair of skates of a much later date, found in 1879, in
an old house in Coppergate. They are nearer to the skates
of the present day, but the steel is much longer.

c. A number of bone implements sharpened at one end,
resembling awls or prickers. Their age and use are unknown.
These were found in the Old Malton culvert, others have
occurred in York.—*The Monkman Collection*, 1875.

d. Some curiously carved bones found near Heworth in
1879. Another has since been found in York. Several
similar bones may be seen in the Guildhall Museum, London.

e. A large number of curious objects found under a house
in Goodramgate in 1878, and probably Danish. They consist
of fragments of pottery, spindle-whorls, implements in iron,
bone, and stone.

f. A series of axe-heads of various ages upon a stand.

g. A large stand covered with articles in iron of various
kinds and periods, found in York, such as knives, shears,
spears, etc., etc.

h. Horse-shoes from Roman times downwards.

i A hammer dredged from the river, 1879 ; a mason's
mallet found under the Bird in Hand Inn, 1878 ; two boat-
anchors from the river Derwent at Malton, 1875, etc.

j. Two boxes of gold-weights, of German work, 16th
century.

* *cf.* Coll. Antiqua, I. 167 ; also the Lincoln Vol. of the Arch. Inst. xxviii. xxxii.

k. Small lockets, or money-boxes of brass. One of them was dredged from the river in 1879, and contains a half-penny of Henry V,, which was found in it.

l. Two larger brass money-boxes. One was found near the City Wall in 1874, and contained a silver penny of Edward IV. and a copper French coin, which were found in it.

m. A small pendant with the arms of England upon it, and several similar objects.

n. An iron marking iron, found at Salley Abbey, with the arms of the borough of Ripon upon it, and RIPON.—*Mr. Walbran's Collection,* 1872.

II. D. *a.* Knives and forks of various ages. A knife and fork, carried originally in a case and used when travelling, with ivory handles veined with silver, etc.—*Mr. Thos. Smith, Huntington Hall,* 1825. A small handle beautifully ornamented.—*Mr. Danby,* 1841. Two pairs of silver handled knives and forks, bought in York, 1881.

b. Knives, etc., of various ages, found in York.

c. A number of spoons from York, of brass or pewter, with deep wide bowls, sæcc. xvi., xvii. The end of one is cut obliquely off, or slipped ; others are ornamented with acorns, trefoils, etc. At the end of one is a print, like a wheel, used for cutting and crimping pastry. Among them is an Apostle spoon of silver, with St. Andrew on the top. A set of these twelve spoons is very rarely to be met with and is of great value.—*Rev. R. Croft,* 1824.

d. Iron hinges of doors from York and Ripon ; a door-handle plate from Ripon.

e. A very large collection of keys from early times downwards. Some of these are probably Roman, as it is almost impossible to distinguish them from those which are more recent.

f. Brass tire from an old chest.

g. Brass tobacco boxes of Dutch manufacture, with embossed figures, made in the 17th century. One presented by Mr. Baker in 1839; another bought in Selby, 1873; two others purchased in York, 1880-1.

h. Tobacco pipes and bowls, with the maker's name stamped thereon, all found in York, where they are very common, and of the 17th and 18th centuries.*

i. Wig-curlers; little round implements of white, baked clay, used for curling hair and wigs.† They are common in York.

j. Two snuff-graters of wood; instruments for making snuff. Bought in York, 1879.

k. Cork-screws of various shapes, in use in the last century. Bought in York, 1879.

l. Nut-crackers, used in the last century.

m. i. The framework of an aulmonière or pouch, which was worn as an appendage to the girdle during the reigns of Henry VII. and VIII. The pouch was of leather, velvet, or ornamented silk, and was fastened to the framework and worn on a girdle, from which it was suspended by a ring. The bar, of brass, is inscribed *Ave Maria grcia ple (sic)*, on the shield in the centre, *Ihs*, and on the other side, *Dominus tecum*, with the letter *W.* in the centre.—*Rev. W. V. Harcourt*, 1823. ii. Part of a similar framework, quite plain.

n. Clasps, etc., and other brass work used in binding MSS. and protecting the sides from injury, used in the library of the Prior and Convent of Durham.—*Rev. J. Raine*, 1881.

o. A circular brooch of silver, with a knight in enamel, dimidiated. A penny of Henry III. was found with it in 1874, near the New Goods Station.

p. i. A handle of a spoon, in lead, with a crest, a six-pointed star surmounted by a coronet. ii. A small object in

* *cf* Journal Arch. Assn., xl. 75
† *cf.* Journal Arch. Inst., vii. 397.

lead like the handle of a spoon, found in the river in 1879, and stamped ᴵꟷ.

r. Several clasps from boxes or coffers found in York.

s. Several small baskets on a stand, from the Hargrove Collection.

t. Several bells, for horses or dogs.

u. A small cup of *cinque cento* work.—*The Cook Collection*, 1872.

v. A charger of latten, lacquered, with St. George and the Dragon upon it, and an illegible inscription. These chargers have frequently been used for alms dishes.—*The Hargrove Collection*, 1847.

w. A large brass horn, probably that with which one of the four Serjeants of the Sheriffs of York used to blow the *Youle girthe* (Christmas feast) at the four bars of the City, on St. Thomas's Day.—*E. H. Roper and William North, Sheriffs of York*, 1839.

x. An ivory horn, the history of which is unknown. It is certainly as early as the 16th century, and has upon it various, almost defaced initials, as if it had belonged to some public body, or had been the yearly prize of some company of archers, each person who became the keeper leaving upon it his initials.

III. D. *a.* Several specimens of fine carving in stone or alabaster, deposited here for security. Two heads of a king and queen found in the Bedern in 1853.—*Purchased.* ii. Two figures in alabaster from the river near St. Mary's Abbey,—*The Hargrove Collection*, 1847. iii. A figure of an angel found in Coney-street in 1880.—*Purchased.* iv. A small font, and a curious head. v. Part of an imperfect alabaster figure, found near Ouse Bridge, in the river.—*The Hargrove Collection*, 1847. vi. A singularly beautiful figure of the Virgin and child, seated on a leaf, cut in Derbyshire marble, and found near the Foss in 1879. vii. Part of a curious stone found in Petergate in 1879, which has probably been used by a sculptor to assist him in forming mediæval letters.

III. D. *b.* On a large stand are the following specimens of Christian art. i. A very fine enamelled plate of Limoges work, 10½in. by 5½in., of the 12th or 13th century, which has served probably as a cover to a copy of the Four Gospels. It represents the Saviour seated on a rain-bow and surrounded by an aureole. The usual symbols of the Evangelists are at the corners. These figures are in relief and are formed of several pieces of metal, richly gilt and affixed to the plate : the eyes are made of enamel.—*Mr. James Atkinson*, 1823.

ii. A similar plate, 8½in. by 4in., representing the Saviour on the cross, with His Mother and St. John. Below is a prostrate figure in the act of prayer ; above are two angels ; and on the upper limb of the cross the monograms xps. ihs.— *Rev. Benedict Rayment*, 1826.

iii. A figure of our Lord in ivory, of 17th century work, found at Sculcoates. *Purchased*, 1873.

iv. An enamelled cross of Byzantine design and covered with inscriptions and monograms.—*Mr. J. Barber*, 1834.

v. A small plaque representing the Crucifixion, found near Tang Hall.—*Mr. T. S. Noble*, 1875.

vi. A larger plaque, representing the visit of the Angels to Abraham and Sarah.

vii. Several small and very early figures in bronze ; one is the Virgin and Child.

viii. A silver brooch found in the church of St. Mary the Less, Durham, and inscribed iesvs nazarenvs rey. Of 14th century work.—*Rev. J. Raine.* A similar brooch, with a doubtful inscription, from York, is near.—*The Browne Collection*, 1878. A small, inscribed gold brooch, found at Fylingdales.—*Mr. G. W. J. Farsyde*, 1857.

ix. A leaden ampulla, one of the various signs or tokens given or sold to those who in the middle ages made pilgrimages to the shrines of saints, and worn by them on the hat, or some part of their garments, as testimonials of their devotion, and partly perhaps as charms. The pilgrim to whom this belonged had visited the shrine of Thomas à Becket, at Canterbury ; who is represented here as wearing his mitre, holding his pastoral staff, and standing beneath a canopy, or perhaps a representation of his shrine at Canterbury. On a thin band, attached to the ampulla, is inscribed OPTIMUS EGRORUM MEDICVS FIT THOMA BONORVM. " Thomas is made the best physician of the virtuous sick." On the other side, of which an etching is exhibited in the case, are represented two priests attending a sick person in bed. In other specimens the murder of Becket by the four knights is represented.* The date of this relic is assigned to the first half of the 13th century.†

x. Beside this curious object is another, bearing the letter T. for Thomas upon it.—*The Browne Collection*, 1878.

xi. A flask of St. Menas, in pottery,‡ found in York. The shrine of this Saint was near Alexandria.

Another pilgrim's bottle, of lead.—*From the Hargrove Collection*, 1847.

xii. Several pilgrim's signs, *a.* small silver horn, surrounding a disk, on which is the legend of St. Hubert. *b.* A tiny equestrian figure of a knight, enamelled.—*Rev. R. Croft*, 1824. *c.* A small roundlet of lead, bearing a cross, found in the York Cemetery.

xiii. On the same stand is part of the handle of a knife carved in ivory, sæc. xv., representing St. John holding the

* Forgeais, Plombs Historiés, p. 140.

† Sse C. R. Smith's Collect. Antiq. i, p. 81; ii. 43, etc. Journal of Archæol. Assoc., i. 200, and v. 125, etc., with an engraving.

‡ *cf.* Smith's Christian Antiquities *sub voce* Pottery.

poisoned cup, with the eagle at his feet.—*The Cook Collection,*
1872. A small piece of metal work, found in Durham,
inscribed *Pense bien.*

c. A ventilator of lead, in the shape of a diamond, with
elegant tracery,—inserted sometime in the window of a church,
probably the Minster. *Mr. Browne's Collection,* 1878.

d. A curious amulet or magical square in silver, with an
inscription in Hebrew, found in 1829, on the removal of
Layerthorpe bridge, close to the ancient Jewish cemetery.*—
Mr. W. W. Hargrove, 1866.

e. Some fragments of the vestments of an Ecclesiastic, in
cloth of gold, taken from a tomb in the north wall of the nave
of York Minster, close to the door of St. Sepulchre Chapel.
This tomb has been traditionally ascribed to Archbishop
Roger, who died in 1181, but is certainly of a far more recent
date.—*From Mr. Browne's Collection,* 1878.

f. A jewelled tag or pendant to a dress sæc. xvi., and one
or two smaller objects.

g. A chalice of latten, which has been buried with some
Ecclesiastic.

h. A leaden *bulla* of Antonius Grimanus, Doge of Venice,
found in York in 1858. On the obverse is a figure of St. Mark
with *S. M. Venet,* and also, the Doge, with *Ant. Griman.
Dux.* On the reverse, is the Doge's title, *Antonius Grimanus
Dei gra Dux. Venetiar,* etc.

i. A number of the *bullæ* or leaden seals appended by the
Popes to their most important official documents. On the
obverse are the heads of SS. Peter and Paul. The following
Popes are represented in the series: Gregory VIII. (1187).
Found at Cawood.—*Rev. W. V. Harcourt,* 1823. Innocent

* Engraved and described in Margoliouth's History of the Jews in Britain, i. 298.
See also, the Translations of the Y.P.S., and Notes and Queries, 6th S. i., June
12th, 1880, p. 482.

III. (1198—-1216).—*Mr. J. Browne's Collection*, 1877.
Honorius III. (1216—1227). Found in a coffin in Market
Street, having been probably attached to an indulgence.—*The
Hargrove Collection*, 1847. Gregory XI. (1227—41). Alex-
ander IV. (1254—61). Found at Bishopthorpe.—*Rev. W.
V. Harcourt*, 1828. Gregory X. (1271--6).—*Mr. J.
Browne's Collection*, 1877. Innocent V. Found at Helperby.
Bought in York, 1878. Nicolas III. (1277—81).—*Mr.
Rutter, York*, 1840. Nicolas IV. (1288—92). Found in
York.—*Mr. E. Swaine*, 1876. John XXII. (1816—34).
Found in the river Wear at Durham.—*Rev. J. Raine*, 1876.

f. A leaden weight dredged up from the Ouse, 1879,
showing a crowned fleur-de-lis.

k. A number of *matrices* of seals, chiefly Ecclesiastical,
with impressions in wax. i. A small oval seal bearing two
hawks *dos a dos*, and inscribed s. ROBERTI LE VEINER. Found
in York.—*Mr. J. Browne's Collection*, 1877. ii. A similar
seal, with a lion passant, and s. IOH'IS DE CVNINGISTV'. Found
in York.—*From the same Collection.* iii. Another, with two
birds, and SIGILLVM SECRET'. iv. An oval seal, with a hawk
and a hand, and s. RIC' FIL' IOH' POTAGE. v. A small seal
found in Micklegate in 1876 and inscribed s. HUGONIS DE SELBI.
A Hugh de Selby was mayor of York in 1230. vi. The seal
of the Collegiate Church of Hemingbrough, near Selby, representing a master seated and a scholar *sub ferula.* The legend
is s. CAPITVLI DE HEMIGBVRGH.—*Mr. Joseph Hunter, F.S.A.*,
1826. vii. A large, round seal, showing the Virgin and
Child, and the legend VIRGO PVDICA, PIA, NOSTRI MISERERE,
MARIA. This has been ascribed to St. Mary's abbey, and
also to Meaux abbey in Holderness. This seal was given by
Samuel Smith, of York, to Thoresby the antiquary; out of
his museum it went to Dr. Burton, and from him to Francis
Smith, F.S.A., of Newbuilding.—Given to the Musem in

1824 by *Mr. R. Dalton.* viii. An impression in lead of the conventual seal of Hayles abbey, found at Acaster Malbys. It shows the Virgin and Child and is inscribed SIGILLV' FRATER-NITAT' MONASTICE BEATE MARIE DE HAYLES.—*Mr. Hether-ington,* 1860. ix. Another lead seal of an abbey in Germany, with a bishop holding a crozier and book, and inscribed S. CONVENTVS ECCL SCI MARTINI IN MOXSTAT.—*Rev. J. Raine.* x. and xi. Two small oval seals with the pelican in her piety, exactly the same. The legend is SVM PELLICANVS DEI. One of these was found in Blossom Street, and was presented by *Mr. John Prest in* 1847 ; the other is from the *Hargrove Collection,* 1847. xii. A pretty, oval seal, showing our Saviour bearing the cross, and inscribed IHESUS MARIA.—*Mr. Joseph Hunter, F.S.A.,* 1826 ? xiii. A seal bearing the emblems of the Trinity, and inscribed S. ECC. TRINITATIS DE WALCVBYNO. Found in Bolton priory in Craven.—*Rev. Wm. Carr.* xiv. A seal with figures and canopies and S. CAPITULI BEATE MARIE DE SANCTO SPHAIO. Found at Skelton, near York.—*Mr. Charles Robinson, of Rydale,* 1823.

l. A small stand with seals of arms, and monograms, etc. Among the coats of arms is that of Sir Hugh Smithson, Duke of Northumberland, from the Collection of Mr. R. Davies. Two steel seals of arms of the families of Haydock of Pheasant Ford, in Lancashire and Cawthorne, presented by Dr. Gibson, in 1878. Two silver seals of arms, Carleton and Baildon (?), bought in York, 1879 ; another with the bearing of Goateley, also bought in York, 1876; another with a double-headed eagle, and several other seals, some with initial and merchants' marks.

m. A mould or cast in copper of the obverse of a large medal of Elizabeth, daughter of James I. of England, who married Frederick V., Count Palatine. The inscription has been *Elizabetha fil. Ja. Re. Mag. Brit. Fra. et Hi. ux.*

Prin. Fre. V. Com. Pal. El. Du. Ba., i.e., *Elizabeth, daughter of James King of Great Britain, France and Ireland, wife of Prince Frederick V., Count Palatine, Elector, Duke of Bavaria.* This medal, in silver, is in the British Museum.—*Mr. John Seymour*, 1851.

n. A small Collection of finger and signet rings, in various metals. Among these are several betrothal rings. One of gold found in York in 1873 and given by Mr. H. Oakeley, with the posy *Ami vostre amur me lie ;* one of silver, inscribed *Friendship ;* a third, *Let Vertue guide us,* found near Ripon, and purchased 1873 ; a guard ring, with *Amor* in raised panels, found in Walmgate in 1876.

A fine gold ring, sæc. xv., with St. Anne and the Blessed Virgin in *Niello,* found in St. George's Fields, 1881. Another gold ring set with a crystal, found under the new War Office buidings, 1877.

Signet rings of various kinds—one inscribed i.s., was found in St. Leonard's Place in 1834.—*Mr. R. Davies.* Another, bearing the letter *r,* of 15th century work, comes from Fountains abbey, and was perhaps the signet of Abbat John de Ripon.—*Purchased,* 1873.

A small prayer-ring, sæc. xvi., with an inscription to the Blessed Virgin, found at Knapton, near Malton.—*Mr. Robert Tuke,* 1831. A pretty jet ring, inscribed *Now or never.*

o. A stand covered with *matrices,* or impressions of seals. Among the latter is one of the Great Seal of Henry VII., given by Mr. J. Brookbank in 1834 ; and one of the fine seal of Ferdinand III., Emperor of Germany, given by the Rev. J. Raine. Among the *matrices* is a fine armorial seal of *Gorge Rygmayden,* showing over the shield of arms a maiden, *rigged out.** This seal was found at Southwell, and was presented by Archbishop Harcourt in 1829. An armorial seal of Thomas

* *cf.* Arch. Journal, ii. 188.

Bolde, bought in Durham and presented by Rev. J. Raine in 1873. Another fine armorial seal, which belonged to the late Mr. Davies ; the surname of the owner is illegible. A jet seal of Almond de Bowes, which is probably a forgery.* A small seal of Richard de Bristou, or Bristol, with a merchant's mark, presented by Mr. T. S. Noble in 1873. Several small personal seals from Mr. Hargrove's Collection, 1847.

p. A skippet, or ancient box for deeds, made of leather, softened in hot water and then stamped, called *cuir-bouilli*. It is ornamented with animals and foliage, and is supposed by the late Sir S. R. Meyrick to be of the time of Edward II. The dotted ground-work appears to have been filled in with red colour.†—*The Hargrove Collection*, 1847. A similar skippet, plain, and much more recent.

q. A round box or case, probably to hold the pens, etc. of a scribe, prettily stamped, and bearing the following inscription : *Edward Hawke: Love God thy Maker : 1605 : Disce mori mundo, vivere disce Deo.*—*Mr. T. S. Noble*, 1881.

r. On a large stand are exhibited a number of ancient deeds and seals, as specimens, chiefly, of writing from the 12th to the 15th centuries, principally bequeathed to the Society by Mr. Eustathius Strickland. Among these, are grants, under seal, from Adam and Peter de Brus to the priories of Gisborough and Rievaulx, Adam de Newmarch, Sir Alexander Percy of Ormsby, and Maude Countess of Cambridge. The document in the centre is an award made in 1226, in a dispute between the prior and convent of Gisborough and the prior and convent of Watton.

IV. D. *a.* On another large stand are more specimens of ancient writing, and impressions of seals. In the centre

---

* *cf.* Journal Arch. Assn., xiv. 335, for a notice of forged jet seals.

† Engraved and described in Journal Arch. Assn. iii. 123 ; and *cf.* Journal Arch. Inst. xxviii. 141, etc.

is a fine document called a Jesse Roll, an abridged history of the world, brought from Italy by Mr. Taylor How, of Stondon Place, Essex.*—*Rev. E. W. Stillingfleet*, 1865.

A grant of free warren in Brayton, South Duffield, and Barley from Edward III. to Wm. Basset, with a part of the great seal.—*Mr. Thomas Barstow of Gurrow Hill*, 1829. Another deed, with the seal of Richard III., and another with the great seal of Elizabeth. A deed with the later seal of the Merchant Adventurers, York. A most delicately written and illuminated roll in Sanscrit.—*Colonel Markham, Becca Hall*, 1834.

b. Various candlesticks, etc. Among these are : i. Two prick candlesticks, sæc. xiv., finely enamelled with coats of arms, found in 1859, under the floor of the church of St. Mary, Bishophill Senior.—*Purchased.* ii. A smaller candlestick of the same kind, found under the new Bank buildings in Market Street.—*Purchased*, 1873. iii. A bronze candlestick, found whilst draining at Benningbrough.—*Hon. Payan Dawnay*, 1858. iv. A brass candlestick and snuffers. At the top of the snuffers is a female figure, armed with a sword and shield and bearing a cross ; and above the head two cherubs holding a wreath. This is probably of early 16th century work.—*Rev. R. Croft*, 1824. v. Various other candlesticks, snuffers, tinder-boxes, a lantern used in the minster last century, and a large link bought in York in 1880.

c. A pewter alms-dish, silvered, inscribed : *St. Martin-le-Grand. Ex dono John Yeates gen. 1675.*—*Purchased in York*, 1879.

d. Two staves or maces, borne in state before a sheriff, and richly carved and coloured. i. This has on it the arms of Langley of Wykeham abbey, and may have been used either

---

* This is a document of some historical interest. There is a letter about it from Mr. Taylor How to Thomas Gray the poet, in Mason's Life of Gray (1st ed.) p. 380, and, with enlargements, in Mitford's edn. of Gray's Works, ii. pp. 421—9.

by Boynton Langley, who was High-Sheriff in 1763; or by his son, Richard Langley, who filled the same office in 1786. This staff belonged to Mr. Davies.—*Rev. A. S. Porter*, 1880. ii. A smaller staff, bearing the arms of Ellis, and probably used by William Ellis, who was one of the Sheriffs of the city in 1796.

e. A brass coffin-plate, purchased by the late Mr. Charles Monkman at Ganton, near Scarbro', bearing the following inscription:— "*Here lyeth the body of Mrs. Eliz. Wharton, wife to ye Honed. Phillip Wharton, Esq., daughter and heiresse to Richd. Hutton, Esq., who departed this life on ye 30th day of March, in ye 29th yeare of her aye, Anno Dom. 1684.*" This is said to have been taken from some church near Malton. · It is more probable that it came from Edlington, near Doncaster, where the Whartons lived, and where the husband of the lady thus recorded was buried.—*The Monkman Collection*, 1875.

f. Two sheaths for knives of stamped leather, or *cuir bouilli*, found in 1873 under the new Bank buildings in Market Street, and the top of a small box, of the same material, from the Croft Collection.

g. Early combs. That imbedded in lime was taken out of a wall adjacent to the King's Manor, and was probably dropped into the wet mortar out of the pocket of some early mason. A similar comb dredged from the river, 1879. The handle of a walking stick, of horn, shaped like a bird.

h. Several pairs of shoe-buckles of the last century, etc.

i. On a stand. An incident in the life of King David in tapestry work.—*Exhibited by Mrs. Norcliffe.* An old sampler made by Mary Field in 1716.—*Purchased in York*, 1871.

j. A very finely chased watch of copper-gilt made in 1640, with the motto, *Nescis qua hora, vigila.*—*Rev. R. Croft*, 1824. ii. A similar watch, richly enamelled, and probably of French manufacture, of the age of Louis the XIV.—*Mr. W. Rudston-Read*, 1875. A silver-gilt scent-bottle with a medal of William and Mary let into the side.—*The same donor.*

k. A number of articles of ladies' dress, etc., during the last century, such as fans, high-heeled shoes, purses, waist-buckles, a necklace and earrings given by Dr. Gibson in 1878. Among them is a fine miniature of a gentleman, which has long been in the possession of the Society.

Pins, needles, thimbles, an old ticket to the York Grand Stand from Sheriff Hutton Park, and various other curiosities.

On the wall of the room, in a frame, is a square of ancient tapestry, representing the arms of Scrope, surrounded by what was called a trail of leaves and flowers. This is a fragment of a set of hangings originally used in the choir of the Minster, and given by the Scrope family in the 15th century. They were removed in the last century and placed in the old Deanery. This fragment had got into lay hands and was saved from destruction a few years ago : another fragment is in the vestry of the Minster.

J. SAMPSON, PRINTER, CONEY-STREET, YORK

www.ingramcontent.com/pod-product-compliance
Lightning Source LLC
Chambersburg PA
CBHW030846270326
41928CB00007B/1248